William James Stillman

Herzegovina and the late uprising

the causes of the latter and the remedies, from the notes and letters of a special

correspondent

William James Stillman

Herzegovina and the late uprising
the causes of the latter and the remedies, from the notes and letters of a special correspondent

ISBN/EAN: 9783337017798

Printed in Europe, USA, Canada, Australia, Japan

Cover: Foto ©ninafisch / pixelio.de

More available books at **www.hansebooks.com**

HERZEGOVINA

AND THE LATE UPRISING:

THE CAUSES OF THE LATTER

AND THE REMEDIES.

FROM THE NOTES AND LETTERS OF A SPECIAL

CORRESPONDENT.

BY W. J. STILLMAN,

AUTHOR OF " THE CRETAN INSURRECTION
OF 1866-8," &c., &c.

LONDON:

LONGMANS, GREEN, AND CO.

1877.

PREFACE.

OF the numerous maps which the events of the past year and a half have called out, unfortunately, there is not one which, in the region particularly involved by the operations of the insurrection in **Herzegovina**, is trustworthy in its details. The best is that of the Austrian Staff; but even this, in the mountain region about Baniani, &c., is extremely inaccurate. That of Kiepert is in general clear and correct, but apparently has not been founded on actual survey in any of the sections bordering on Montenegro. The only entirely accurate one of this section is that made for the Montenegrin Government, but never published. For a general notion of the relations of Dalmatia and Montenegro to Herzegovina—the exposition of which has been one of the principal objects of my book—any of the maps will suffice, and the military strategy hardly requires explanation.

The question of pronunciation of Slav names is one which seems to create a confusion I cannot flatter myself I shall be able to clear up. For the final syllable of all patronymic, &c., names, ordinarily written as *ich* or *itch*, the latter method, clumsy though it seems, is the only one which leaves no doubt as to the approximate sound; but, as this combination represents three recognized sounds in the Serb language, we can *only* approximate. In the Croatian these three are represented by the letter *c* with accents. This simple expedient is forbidden by our scholastic traditions; and in my spelling I have had recourse to a form which is as capable as the *ich* of being mispronounced—viz., *ics;* but the soft sound of *ch* qualified by *s* will give the nearest approach to the sound I can contrive. The triple *c*, represented in the Cyrilian alphabet by three letters, is incommunicable by English signs. The nearest idea I can give is as *cs*, as above, *jh*, and *ch* as in rich. The name of the town which I have written Niksics has thus been printed:—Nicksitch, Nichsitch, Nicsich, Niksic, Nichsic, Nichsich, and Niksics. The " Illyrian " is Niksić. The final consonant is always soft, whatever may be the spelling.

INTRODUCTORY.

THE principal purpose of publishing this fragment of history is to place in clearer light certain motives and causes for the Herzegovinian insurrection which are not generally accepted by, or were not visible to, the general public, and which were hardly to be given in journalistic narrative while events were in progress, either because learned subsequently, or because they became known to me rather from regard for a certain reputation acquired in years gone by, during an insurrection in Crete, of being a sympathizer and active friend of the Rayahs, than because I was correspondent of an English journal; and in some cases were only open to me on the understanding that they were not to be alluded to in correspondence.

Having been in 1866-8 thoroughly conversant with the Turkish manner of making war under similar circumstances, and personally acquainted with many Turkish functionaries, civil and military, I had, naturally, formed very decided opinions as to the merits of that struggle between humanity and the desire for progress on one side and barbarism and an intolerable oppression on the other, which is the element of uncertainty in what is known as the Eastern question. If the

having entered the field with these opinions, so defined, dis-
qualified me for the office of a candid historian, my readers
must judge. I am conscious of no bias but that which my
painful and costly experience of Turkish customs and character has enforced me to, and I have endeavoured in my
narration to avoid all discoloration of the events; as to
the sympathies with which I followed them, I imagine no
really unprejudiced person could expect that they would not
be on the side which was substantially right, and which had
every claim to the sympathy of right-minded men.

As events are hurrying on, my story may be useless as a
lesson before even it is printed—at least, it is to be hoped
that the civilized world will never be called on again to ad-
judicate between the Rayah and his master; but even so, it
may be worth while to see how completely the old despotism
is responsible for its own downfall, and how little any outside
agency had to do with a revolt which might have been
developed at any moment into insurrection, by any circumstance that gave the Rayahs a hope, even momentary; and
how many opportunities to allay it were thrown away.

The condition of the Christian Herzegovinian was the
most intolerable of all the subjects of Turkey, for the
poverty of the country gave little solace for his slavery, and
the nearness of Montenegro and Dalmatia made the contrast
between his condition and that of his near kinsmen the
greater. Certainly in no country in which I have ever been
was the state of life of the people so wretched as his, and
the still not entirely tamed mountain spirit made the endurance of oppression more vexatious, and the eagerness to
seize any opportunity or real encouragement to rise much
more keen.

The visit of the Emperor of Austria to the Dalmatian

coasts (which are the coasts also of Herzegovina), and the marked interest thus for the first time shown in the Slav population of this section, stimulated the ferment continually going on there, and led the Catholic Herzegovinians to anticipate an Austrian intervention. The insurrection in its early stages was mainly amongst the Catholic population between Popovo and Gabella, not less oppressed than the Orthodox, but more controlled by the clergy (who have a lively apprehension of any movement which has its basis in Servian, Russian, or Montenegrin intrigues), but at the same time, far less individual and warlike by reason of this control. The insurrection spread because the whole country was ripe for it, and because the military conduct of the Turks was inefficient and unintelligent, and perversely directed, as far as it went, to provoke rather than subdue or allay the insubordination. Under governments which give no basis or motive for loyalty, insurrection is chronic even if latent ; and under the rule of the Turks, there is never peace, only a truce between conqueror and conquered, in which no law has ever intervened to limit the right of the victor over his victim. It is only the law of force in its first and uncrystallized or uncodified state—an extended brigandage, a long time feared by all Europe, and since respected as a *fait accompli*, with the respect men pay to the work of four centuries, even when, as in this case, that work is in itself utterly evil. This truce is liable at all times to be broken by any individual Mussulman on his own responsibility,—a condition which naturally involves the corresponding one of a readiness of the Rayah to revolt at all times.

Every incident therefore which gives a hope of successful revolt, or which increases the normal injustice of the oppression, is at once followed by revolt. Those who have read

the interesting book of Mr. Evans on Bosnia and Herzegovina at the moment of the outbreak will know what was
the ordinary condition of those provinces. The latter has
never been long quiet—the interval of peace since 1862 is
probably the longest which has obtained since the conquest,
and this was probably due to the fact that in the repression of that year the Austrian Government took an active
part, and so efficiently that the impression remained that
nothing was to be done until Austria was favourably disposed. Montenegro even owed the only considerable
defeat of the century past to the merciless blockade which
Austria established along her whole frontier, cutting off
entirely supplies of ammunition, so that in the last battles
between the Turks and Montenegrins the latter had only
five cartridges per man, powder was worth its weight in
silver, and a single percussion cap cost tenpence ! and the
men ceased fighting because they saw that to go into battle
with only their handjars against rifled muskets and artillery,
was an useless sacrifice of life. The Herzegovinian allies
had been conquered by Austrian troops acting with the
Turks—there was no sign of encouragement from any side,
and Servia, in spite of pledges given long before, had taken
concessions from the Porte, and was hopelessly tranquil.

Turkey had therefore been victorious under circumstances which made her victory precarious; she owed it to
Austrian assistance, and achieved it, even at that, with forces
demoralized to a great extent by several bloody disasters,
which only the utter recklessness of human life, which characterized Omar Pasha's strategy, enabled them to retrieve ;
and if the Montenegrins had been able to obtain, even at the
last moment, supplies of ammunition, they would have
turned the event of the war completely, for the Turks had

secured no position of vital importance, and had accomplished only a small part of the work to be done to really conquer Montenegro.[1]

The Cretan insurrection had since that time given the Ottoman empire a blow from which, in its decaying condition, it had never been able to recover. The expenditure of that war—over 50,000 men and £10,000,000 !—was too much for its diminishing vitality to recuperate, while the Mussulman populations had become equally demoralized by the disastrous drain on their able-bodied men. Towards the end of the Cretan insurrection the soldiers who were being embarked for Crete were so infected with the dread of this service that desertions were very numerous and disaffection general,[2] and the supreme effort which the Porte has since made to meet the Servian revolt and create a religious enthusiasm has not restored the old *morale* of the Mussulman population, or effaced the great discouragement which the Cretan insurrection produced. And whatever may have been the case with the Turkish troops before Alexinatz, and against the Servians, I have no kind of hesitation in saying that in Herzegovina and before the Montenegrin lines they showed anything but good *morale*—such, in fact, as could only be found with decaying military power, their best battalions

---

[1] Omar Pasha in his reports pretended to have reached Cettinje, but in fact his army was never in sight of that place, and the positions to be taken before reaching it were so strong that his army, enfeebled as it was, would possibly have been unable to reach it even against the discouraged resistance of the Montenegrin force. Omar himself said at Constantinople to a friend of mine, that if the Prince had sent 5,000 fresh men against his army when it had reached Rieka he could not have offered an effectual resistance, and would have been obliged to abandon his conquest.

[2] See Blue book on Cretan insurrection, despatches of Consul at Beyrout.

not being comparable to those which came to Crete in 1867, while the mismanagement and demoralization in the higher ranks were still more striking. I feel confident, looking at the matter with impressions not materially modified since then, that the Cretan insurrection made the Herzegovinian revolt practicable and successful, and that from the two the independent existence of the Ottoman empire is henceforward impossible, even if Russia should not succeed in breaking it down completely. The Slavs have been progressing in political knowledge as well as moral force, in spite of oppression, and the Mussulmans have followed the usual course of nations which govern without regard to justice or political economy, and destroy the sources of their own power, growing weaker and less coherent with each generation, according to the law

"Which makes the crime its own blindfold redresser."

I have purposely avoided any mention of the agitation in Bosnia, not only because I saw nothing of it, but because it was evidently a reflection from that in the Herzegovina, and had never any great force or coherence. In Croatia, however, it presented the peculiarity that it showed the pugnacity and irrepressibility of the Catholics, as in Herzegovina it did that of the Orthodox Christians.

CHAPTER I.

N arriving at Trieste at the end of August, 1875, I found that there was very little knowledge of, or interest in, the Herzegovinian movement there. Bands were known to be hanging about Klek, Trebinje, and Zubci, but there seemed to be nothing known of the upper Herzegovina. Two or three bands were formed in Piva, Baniani, and other districts on the immediate borders of Montenegro, in which was a certain element of Montenegrins proper, and many Crivoscians (Austrian subjects from the Bocche di Cattaro), most of which were under the command of Herzegovinians, the sole exception being that of Peko Pavlovics, an old Montenegrin Turk-fighter, whose courage had been tried in more than sixty battles, and whose presence was an unfailing element in any war or revolt against the Ottoman empire on or near the borders of Montenegro.

There was a committee at Trieste for aiding the movement by supplying arms and forwarding volunteers. The greatest deficiency was that of arms and ammunition, and the Trieste committee could at that time only send old muzzle-loaders of all models, contributed more than purchased. There was no concert and no plan as to any definite object in the insurrection, and all the animus I could perceive was the chronic sympathy with a people who were known to be grossly oppressed, and who were fighting against their masters. What political tone I could find was distinctly Austrian, and the members of the committee were all Dalmatians, with whom, as with the Dalmatian patriots generally, the best end of the affair would be the union of Bosnia and part, at least, of Herzegovina to Dalmatia. There was no Russian leaning or influence.

My Cretan experience hardly left me to conjecture on the immediate causes of discontent, and inquiry going down the coast, and wherever I saw any of the local committees, confirmed, circumstance by circumstance, the old story. The Christian had neither justice, security, nor the common rights of humanity. No court sat for him, but all against him; no tenure of land held against the declaration of a Mussulman, and even the sanctity of the family was constantly invaded by the carrying off of the young girls for the harems of their masters. Everywhere and from the lips of the most dispassionate men I heard the same confirmations. In Bosnia the slavery was more abject, but in Herzegovina the population was poorer and less able to support exactions like those endured by the Bosnian, and the energy with which the Herzegovinian occasionally resists extreme oppression made it not so safe to the Mussulman; so that on the whole Herzegovina was less repressed than Bosnia. Perhaps the downright killing of Christians was more common in the former province, but, in revenge, more Mussulmans were made to pay this last penalty of a law which comes sometimes to redress lawlessness; and so a certain balance was struck.

A single case of judicial injustice, one of whose victims I saw and questioned, and of which I obtained ample confirmation at Mostar, may be adduced as a sample of the

status quo which we have been often told leaves no real
justification for insurrection. A certain young man from the
neighbourhood of Trebinje had, in a quarrel, killed an Aga,
and fled to Montenegro. His nearest male relations[1] were
therefore arrested, to the number of six, and thrown into
prison, being tortured in various ways to compel confession
of complicity; two being put in long wooden boxes, like
coffins, and rolled downhill, others being stood upright with
their heads in a hole in the floor of the prison, which allowed
them to rest on their shoulders, having splinters of wood
driven under their finger-nails (the boy I saw in Ragusa gave
a minute account of the operation, sickening in its fidelity
to detail). The father of the murderer died in prison, and
one of the cousins was taken out of the prison in Mostar,
just five days before the Consular Commission arrived, and
hung before one of the mosques to calm the excitement of
the Bashi-bazooks, the ruffians who, to show their sense of
such occasional luxuries, had, in the beginning of the war,
planned a general massacre of the Christians of Mostar, and
were only dissuaded from their scheme by being assured by
one of the more prudent Agas that such a feat would only
result in the Austrian army taking possession of the country.

In general when any Herzegovinian became obnoxious to
the authorities, or, which amounted to the same thing, to the
Agas or Beys, he fled to Montenegro, if he could escape.
I have heard several incidents described as the immediate
cause of the outbreak, but the fact is that there was scarcely

[1] The practice of imprisoning or otherwise punishing relatives of an
offender who cannot be captured is universal in all Turkish jurisprudence. I myself came across cases of it in Crete, perpetrated by Ismael
Pasha, a highly reputed functionary, who had been educated in Paris.
I believe that every impartial European consul in the whole empire will
have known cases of the same abuse of power.

a district in Herzegovina which had not sent its representatives
to that city of refuge, the free Montenegro.   In one village
three Turks had violated two women, and the relatives had
killed one or more of the violators, and, with their immediate
male relatives, fled to the usual asylum ; in another, a man
had resisted illegal collection of taxes, and killed an official
who attempted to levy them by force ; another was driven
out of the country by attempts to kill him as a dangerous man
—*i.e.*, one who had a great moral influence on his fellow
villagers (of this Socica was a remarkable case) ; and one of
the most prominent incidents in this flint, steel, and gun-
powder arrangement was that of a local tax farmer at
Nevesinjè, who, on occasion of the marriage of his son,
attempted to compel his *clientèle* to pay supplementary tax
in the shape of wedding presents,—a form of extortion which
was obstinately resisted, whereupon the farmer sent the
zapties to enforce the levy.   The recusants fled as usual.

The collection of fugitives in the dominions of Prince
Nikita became so serious a consideration, that remon-
strances were made to the Government at Seraievo; and,
after prolonged negotiations, a promise was made to the
Prince, that the exiles should return on guarantees of their
personal safety, and come to Seraievo to discuss their complaints.   Amongst these men were the pope Simonics, since
a prominent leader of the insurgents, from Gatschko, and
Gligor Millecivics of Bilek, also a captain of note.   In consequence of this arrangement, the chief of all the refugees
returned to Herzegovina *viâ* Baniani *en route* for Seraievo,
and were stopped by a patrol of zapties; but the Christians
refusing to recognize the right of arrest, a fight ensued, in
which several of them were killed.   This, of course, drove
the rest back into Montenegro, when the agitation became

serious over the whole province, and a number of the Nevesinjè refugees returned home and began hostilities. Luka Petcovics of Shuma, near Trebinje, an old and experienced insurgent, exiled for many years, came to take part; while from Servia came another exile of the insurrection of 1862, Ljubibratics, who was accompanied by several Servians and Dalmatians.

The then governor, Dervish Pasha, was openly accused of stimulating discontent, in order to distinguish himself in the repression, like Ismael Pasha, in Crete, in 1866. A body of troops, with another of Bashi-bazooks, were sent out, who burned a number of villages, and murdered the people they found on the road, armed or unarmed; and Constant Effendi, an Armenian in the service of the Porte (since more known as Constant Pasha), sent an invitation to the principal malcontents to come to a conference and state their griefs. When they came near the rendezvous, they found Constant Effendi's assembly tent pitched within short range of an old fortification, where was concealed a body of troops; and, accusing him of treachery, they refused to approach nearer, and thus ended this effort at conciliation.

Meanwhile the insurrection had caused anxiety in Montenegro, for the principality was not prepared for an outbreak, to which it could not rest alien, and which would surely draw the Montenegrins in. Peko Pavlovics was sent to pacify it. This the old Turk-fighter did *modo suo* by capturing Ljubibratics, and marching him bodily across the frontier to Ragusa with his hands tied behind his back. I am inclined to think that the matter would have stopped there if the Turks had shown the slightest disposition to conciliation, as the encouraging elements were largely wanting. Russia

was not yet ready, and the whole affair, so far as committees
and moral influence were concerned, was entirely in the
hands of the Austrian Slavs, the committees of Zara and
Ragusa being the chief. The Catholic districts along the
frontier were the most enthusiastic in the revolt, while the
Austrian authorities showed an extraordinary amount of
complaisance to the insurgents. But the Catholics were
tindery fuel, quickly kindled and quickly spent; help did
not come as they had hoped for it, and fighting for themselves was what they were not used to, and all the stimuli of
the friendly Dalmatians were needed to keep the fire up.

According to all the testimony I have been able to collect
from the day of my arrival to the present, there was no difficulty in pacifying the province at this time, and no Government seemed disposed to stimulate the insurrection; and if
the Porte had been capable of securing immunity from personal oppression to the Christian there would have been no
grounds for prolonging it.[1]   Neither Russia nor Montenegro

[1] CONSUL HOLMES TO THE EARL OF DERBY.

My Lord,   *Mostar, September* 24, 1875.

I have the honour to enclose copy of a despatch and its enclosures,
addressed to Sir Henry Elliot on the 10th, just before leaving Mostar to
endeavour to communicate with the insurgents.   At present the departure of the post only allows me time to add that my Russian and French
colleagues and myself returned here on the 22nd, having entirely failed
to persuade the insurgents we met to submit, and to bring their complaints before Server Pasha.   We did not, however, see any of the
principal chiefs of the insurrection, who were all in the neighbourhood
of Trebinje.

Our colleagues of Austria, Germany, and Italy returned on the 23rd,
having been equally unsuccessful.   They, however, saw the leaders of
the insurrection near Trebinje, who demand an armistice, and a European intervention to guarantee the reforms which may be adopted.   I
would here remark that, contrary to what is asserted in so many news-
papers, the people of the Herzegovina neither demand, nor have ever
desired, an impossible autonomy, as Servian agitators would have per-

could be indifferent to any similar movement at any time, but
Russian influence had already suffered too much from previous checks and withdrawals to risk either idle excitement
of insurrection, or indifference to it actually excited. Montenegro may profess neutrality as much as it pleases, but
neutrality in the sense demanded of it, is, and always was,
morally and politically impossible. But Montenegro was in
no position to run the grave risks of war with Turkey,
and though no international obligation held the Prince to
prevent individuals from going into the war, his failure to
do so was a convenient *casus belli*, and his declarations that
he had kept them back were politic indulgences in a species
of evasion which the persistent habit of diplomacy prevents
us from characterizing when practised by governments as
we should if used by individuals. There is no room for
denial that Prince Nikita did allow his subjects to go to
the aid of Herzegovina, and that later many followed
Peko, and that no one was ever punished, but that some
were rewarded by medals for distinguished bravery. But
this does not affect the fact, that at the juncture when Constant Effendi went to meet the insurgent chiefs, and the
Catholic population had become discouraged and abandoned
the war, the Turkish authorities might have pacified the
province *had they been so willed.* But this was perhaps one
of the very incapacities of the Ottoman organization—it
cannot pacify except by force—there is no element of con-

suaded them to do. *They only ask to remain subjects of the Sultan, with
reformed laws, and a proper and just administration of them.* How to
secure this is the difficulty.

Next week I hope to forward a detailed report of my mission, the
failure of which I have already telegraphed to Sir Henry Elliot.

I have, &c.,

(Signed)   W. R. HOLMES.

ciliation or good faith in it ; and Constant Effendi, in trying
to entrap the chiefs, took the only precaution in his power.
The wrong and its consequences had so accumulated, that
perhaps the strain to the system of administration, of doing
justice to so much injustice, would have brought another
explosion in the attempt to avoid this. What was possible
and even probable was, that the refugees should have
returned to Montenegro and Dalmatia, Austria securing
immunity for the Catholics, and things might have been
patched up until another explosion and a riper opportunity.
And this bade fair to be the solution of the affair as its first
phase ended.

At this juncture (Aug. 18) came the Consular Commission.
I do not know to whom its formation is due, but it is tolerably certain that to it was due the reawakening of the insurrection.   It was a partial recognition by the Powers of the
wrongs of the Herzegovinian, and an indication that the
eyes of official Europe were on his state,—sufficient encouragement at any time to make him revolt, and to stimulate the
spirit of combativeness in the mountain regions bordering
Montenegro; and owing to this the whole aspect of the
affair changed rapidly.

When, early in September, I arrived at Ragusa, the preliminary phase of the war was over. The bands that had
been infesting the plain country about Trebinje, nominally
besieging the city, had made only a kind of demonstration.
There were few troops in the place, and the insurgents had
taken up their quarters in the Monastery of Duzi, between
Trebinje and the frontier. As soon as Turkish reinforcements arrived from Stolatz, the monastery was attacked, and
the insurgents, abandoning it, fled across the frontier or to
the mountains. A considerable body of them came across

to Ragusa, and came on board the Lloyd's steamer by which I was a passenger, and proceeding to Castel Nuovo in the Bocche di Cattaro, landed with their arms and crossed the frontier to Zubci, where they had made rendezvous with their companions who, stronger on foot, had made the journey by land. Their arms were openly landed from the steamer, and no questions were asked by any one.

[This was the policy until after the refusal of the insurgents to accept the Andrassy Note the following winter.]

The war in those parts was only a frolic for the volunteers, who went and came as they liked, going to Castel Nuovo for a change from camp-life, the mayor of that city being head of the committee which was charged with the distribution of arms and supplies, and the channel of communication with the world was now by Sutorina.

The so-called siege of Trebinje was merely a *coup de théâtre;* no serious attack had ever taken place, and only in the regions near Montenegro and where an element of Montenegrinism existed in the bands was there any serious fighting. During August Socica had raised the standard in the district of Piva, north of Niksics, and defeated the Turks in several small affairs, destroying many blockhouses, while Peko, finding that peace had not been made by his heroic treatment, and that Ljubibratics had returned, went over to the insurgents, and a number of Montenegrin volunteers, with several hundreds of the pugnacious and Turk-hating Crivoscians, had joined the movement. The whole of Zubci, Yezero, Piva, Gatschko, Baniani, Rudini and Dabra, were under arms, and they possess a population of a different temper from those of Gabella, Popovo, and others bordering on Dalmatia, and are comparatively free from the vexations of the Turkish rule. But, on the other hand, they are exceedingly prone to fight for the sake merely of fighting the Turks.

Great devastation was already being wrought, the Turks burning and destroying everything before them in the lower country, killing and plundering in all the Christian villages, and the insurgents naturally retaliating to their best on the Turkish. The trans-frontier districts were crowded with refugees—old men, women, and children.

In the Bocche di Cattaro there was intense excitement and sympathy for the insurrection. From Crivoscie the whole able-bodied male population had gone to the war, and Zupa[1] prepared to follow. The Bocchesi have always made common cause with their Montenegrin kinsman as well as with the mountain Hezegovinian, being all of the same stock, combative habit, and religion. At Cattaro it was believed that Montenegro was on the point of declaring war, and it was only in Montenegro one could ascertain what was being done.

---

[1] Crivoscie and Zupa are two of the most warlike districts of the Bocche di Cattaro and at opposite ends of the territory, the former bordering on Herzegovina, the latter on Albania.

CHAPTER II.

THE difficult, dizzy road from Cattaro seems to be a great labour for little fruit when, after four hours of climbing, you enter the outermost plain of the Crnagora, and find a few arid acres in the midst of a great amphitheatre of grey, glistening rock, the interstices of which hardly give rooting to a chance shrub. Here and there a dwarfed evergreen is to be seen, and only on one side a strip of forest, of starveling, dwarfed, and gnarled beeches, more like a copse than a forest; but with this narrow exception, all round the circle the desolation is like that of a silent volcano, arid as if internal fires had burnt out the juices of the earth. In little patches here and there along the edge of the hills, where the soil has been held by basins of rock, the husbandman has made his opportunity, and the little walled-in fractions of a rood, some of them not larger than 6 feet by 10 feet, make their best, though poor, return of maize, potatoes, wheat, or grass. Where the space to be reclaimed permits it, the earth is terraced and protected from the wash of the torrents. It is a poor, gravelly soil at best, even in the plains, and little of it, at that, in comparison with the expanse of bare rock, and certainly nothing but liberty could make any people fight for it or care to keep it.

The Valley of Njegush, the natal place of the Prince of

Montenegro, is the first halting-place. A score or two of small stone houses, mostly of two rooms each on the ground floor, with two or three of two stories, one of which was the residence of the family of the Prince, compose the tale of Njegush, the village; and the soil around seemed hardly sufficient to support the few people in it. Few men were to be seen; women carrying heavy loads, and children peering round the corners and doors to watch the unwonted stranger, were all that we saw. To say that the people were poorly dressed is little; the garments of some of them were in tatters already, and in any civilized country they would, most of them, have been better off as beggars. But no one thought himself, or herself, the worse for it, and all saluted us with gravity and respect, but with no trace of servility.

From Njegush to Cettinje the road is still more difficult—from a defensive point of view, much better; and I could hardly avoid the conviction that bad roads are an article of faith with the Montenegrin; he will hardly see the policy of opening his country to artillery with the other modern improvements until his independence is secured by an European guarantee. The road between Njegush and Cettinje is so bad that there are places where one must dismount to descend safely; but in a walk of four hours from the Austrian frontier we enter the Plain of Cettinje, the central plain of the Crnagora proper.

The residence of the ruler of Montenegro is worthy its Lacedæmonian prototype. There is one straight, wide street, with about forty houses on each side, low, stone-built, and covered, some with tiles and some with thatch, and without chimneys; none with more than one floor above the ground, some with only a ground floor, all nearly alike in accommodation and in pretension. In one is the Telegraph and Post-office, in another the Ministry of Communications ; but no external sign indicates any difference between this and the meanest man's home. The end of the street is blocked by a larger house, also of two stories, which was built for an hotel, and which, lately, has been the best I found south of Trieste along the whole Slav country ; and a cross street leads down to the Prince's residence—a plain building which it would be courtesy only to call a palace ; it is merely the largest house in Cettinje. Opposite is the former residence of the Prince, made later a seminary, and then used for the accommodation of the few strangers who came here, the ground floor for Government offices. At the foot of the hills close by is a monastery, without occupants, except one or two old priests ; a few outlying houses, and this is all of Cettinje, except its people. In this, as in the other plains of Montenegro, beside the central village proper, a fringe of occasional houses runs round it built on the hill-slopes for economy of tillable land. Around is the same amphitheatre of grey hills, only here the more friable rock permits the clinging of scanty and impoverished trees in their interstices. The productions of the plain are mainly potatoes and maize, a few trees—either willow, poplar, or mulberry—and opposite the palace one elm-tree of considerable size, beneath which is a circular raised platform of stone, with two or three stone blocks, which serve as seats, and here the Prince administers justice. His body-guard, in the picturesque costume of the whole people, stand or sit around this tree, according as the Prince is present or not, or pass the time in athletic sports on the sward beside it. On meeting the Prince walking, with his guard following or walking beside him, a stranger finds it not easy to distinguish the ruler from his guard. One sees only a mass of three or four score Montenegrins in ordinary costume. They all chat together, and I only learnt which was the Prince by his returning the salute.

There is a simplicity and dignity in the Montenegrin which strikes almost all who know Scotland as resembling strongly the Highlander—grave, taciturn, and yet friendly if occasion offers—canny, soldierlike, and singularly reserved in expression of emotion by any outward sign. The moment was one in which the national temper was tried and displayed to the utmost. Servia had promised to enter the field, and the signal of her movement was to be that for the entry of the Montenegrins into Herzegovina to settle old scores with the Turk. Everybody was anxious to fight, but nobody wished it to appear that he was so—the whole of the three to four hundred men in Cettinje were in the streets, and the only sign of agitation one saw was perpetual movement. There was certainly something grand in this attitude of the smallest independent nation in the bounds of civilization chafing in the leash, and only caring to be free to attack, regardless of consequences or war alliances, its old-time enemy. Nobody thought what Europe or Russia would say or do: they only wanted to know if Servia was going to lead the way, and they be free to move. Finally came the day on which the telegram must arrive which would tell the course Servia was to follow, and one could feel the pulse of the whole principality on that main street, and the approaches to the palace.

The population of Cettinje is not, it is true, large enough to be considered numerically as representing the opinion of Montenegro; but it must be remembered that it includes all the highest functionaries, a body guard of picked men from all the principality, and many persons had come here to

await the decision of the Servian Skuptchina, including
many chiefs of the insurgents. That afternoon these were
all in the streets as if waiting for a proclamation. All along
the side of the street which leads to the palace was a solid
line of men composed of the elements I have named. The
Prince had gone the day before into the mountains—to
hunt wolves, it was said—and that afternoon was to return.
The rumour was current everywhere that **Servia** had yielded
to diplomatic pressure, and that the rising **was** to be abandoned. Dejection **was** on the face of everybody. The
voivodes whom I knew, avoided conversation and **even**
contact, and the Prince's aide-de-camp and those about his
person, who had been in general communicative, kept away
from **us.** I had, however, information enough **to convince**
me that the Prince at an earlier period had had **great pressure**
brought on him by the chiefs of the people to take **up arms**
independently of Servia. It was believed that with armed
neutrality on the part of the Servian Government, and the
passes of Novi Bazaar in the hands of Montenegrins, Klek
could be made good against any force the Turks could
bring against the Christians, and that in this way the few
battalions then in Herzegovina and Bosnia could be
disposed **of before any** great force was brought up to effect
a diversion unless they **were** marched through Servia, the
neutrality of which would thus serve as a potent aid. Meanwhile the insurgents, mixed and disciplined with Montenegrins and armed, would become in a short time an effective
force, increasing the strength of the defence faster than the
attacking force would be increased.

This initiative movement was favoured by some of the
Prince's advisers, and he himself was known to be desirous
of action, so that the temptation to give the word must have

been very great, and, whatever may have been his engagements or apprehensions, he was blamed by many for having
lost an opportunity which might not return.   Of course
Russian influence goes for much, and if Russia had exerted
it in a positive sense, the Prince might have gone into the
war even alone, but Russia was utterly adverse, and I think
I can say with certainty that this influence was then much
weakened, and I heard bitter complaints of repeated disappointment from Russia having on former occasions given
hopes which she took no pains to see fulfilled.   I was told
with acrimony the stories of the old wars when Russia had
drawn Montenegro into war with Turkey, and then made
peace alone, leaving the Montenegrins to the vengeance
of the Turks.   The opinion generally held was that the
moment was the most favourable possible for a general movement, and its loss by diplomatic pressure was to be attributed either to Russian weakness or indifference, for no one
had any very profound faith in a sincere interest on the part
of Russia as to the fortunes of the people of Herzegovina.

It then seemed to me beyond a doubt that if the Powers
should assure Herzegovina a substantial liberty such as was
recommended by "The Times" at the beginning of the
movement, the Prince would gladly accept the solution, and
withdraw his moral influence from the insurgents if they
were inclined to hold out, and this would have been conclusive.   I had the Prince's most earnest assurance that he
would support with all his influence any arrangement
of an equitable nature, which at that moment would have
been decisive, because the withdrawal of such support as the
principality had given would have compelled the submission
of the most formidable section of the insurrection.   The
personal tendencies of the Prince, unlike his predecessors,

were to attain his ends by patience and peaceful appliances if possible, but his people have a very different
way of regarding the matter, and the most that could be
done was, the least possible yielding to the national feeling,
but without losing sight of the national aspirations.

Looking back on the matter after a much fuller acquaintance with Montenegro, I believe that it would have been
unsafe and futile for the Prince to have attempted to cut off
all aid for the insurgents. Thousands of them had fought
for Montenegro in 1858 and 1862, and the strong tendency
of the whole people was to throw itself into the war. The
position of the Prince was a most difficult one. Obliged to
identify himself with his people's feeling, he had no other
control over them than their personal devotion, and must
be careful how he exposed this to too great a strain. At the
same time he must protect his future interest and keep his
influence over the surrounding Slav populations, and as long
as Dalmatian (*i.e.* Austrian) and Servian sympathizers were
in the field for them, it was impossible that Montenegrins
should not be there too, and equally so that they should not
maintain their supremacy of courage and military efficiency,
and I have no hesitation in saying that the Prince would have
endangered his throne sooner or later by indifference to the
struggle in Herzegovina.

As to the public enthusiasm, so utterly damped, it was
easy to estimate it by the dejection which followed the
Servian defection and the pacific decision of the Prince. In
fact, communication became difficult with any of the official
people, and the Prince himself for days would see no one.

Under the circumstances it was of course still more difficult to restrain the Montenegrins, and there is no doubt that
a very considerable increase of personal liberty was conse-

quently accorded. **Before** leaving Cettinje I had an audience of the Prince, in which he expressed freely his disappointment. He most strongly repudiated any Russian direction or dictation, or intention to be pushed by Russia further than his own interests led him. He said that if he should decide to allow any aid to the insurgents compatible with international law, he could maintain it perfectly well until his own funds and supplies were exhausted, and as many of his subjects as he was disposed to give *congé* to, would at once join the insurrection. All this he could easily do without visibly going further than Austria, and the utmost result to him or his country would be, that Turkey would declare war, for which he was quite prepared. The Prince expressed great disappointment at the inaction of Servia, and said that he was ready and willing to move with her had she moved, but that he did not feel justified, in spite of the desire and pressure of his people, in declaring war on Turkey alone. His soldiers were well organized and armed with breechloaders and artillery, whereas in 1862 they had only old-fashioned Albanian smoothbores. His supplies of ammunition were ample, and he did not apprehend defeat in the mountains from all the Turkish troops now in the field ; but the part of a faithful ruler was to spare useless shedding of blood of his people, and he remembered that, though in 1862 they defended their valleys against 60,000 Turks and fought for eight months alone, they were finally obliged to yield to the greater resources of the Porte, their ammunition being exhausted and 3,000 of their number killed without any result whatever ; and if now they were left to fight alone they would probably ultimately meet the same fortune, which he would not take the responsibility of provoking by a declaration of war singly, but his position was such that he could not recoil from any consequence of his strong sympathy, and that of his people, with the Herzegovinians. The event of war might be the same in either case, but while he was willing to risk the event, he was not willing to assume the responsibility before Europe of inviting it by a declaration of war.

He disclaimed any ambition in connection with the insurrection, and was willing, in case the Powers should decide to guarantee an autonomy to the Herzegovinians, to exert his utmost influence towards the speedy cessation of the insurrection, though without some such guarantee being given to the insurgents it would be impossible for him to take any pacificatory action in the matter. The insurgents were a kindred people; they looked to him for his moral support at least, and he could not refuse it. His own people would support him unanimously should he go further even; but in view of all the circumstances he regarded the cessation of bloodshed as the most important object if accompanied by concession of the requisite security of the Rayahs. He said that the mission of the Consuls would be fruitless, because it was based on Turkish promises of redress, and the experience of the people with regard to these promises was such that they had no value whatever in their eyes. He was confident that the insurrection would hold out at least through the winter, which he believed would be very trying to the Turkish troops from warmer regions, as the cold of the mountain districts is very intense, while the mountaineers being accustomed to it would suffer much less. He begged me finally, in case war should break out, which he still regarded as possible, to come up again and accompany him during the campaign.

It was impossible not to sympathize with a ruler placed

in this position, keenly awake to all its dangers and re-
sponsibilities, and devoted to his people with a really
paternal devotion.

I left Cettinje with the feeling of having extended my
own horizon by the discovery of a people of the old heroic
type—a survival of the Homeric age, doubtless with heroic
vices which also survive elsewhere, but with some virtues
which hardly survive the larger civilization. I think that few
Englishmen could resist this impression, and most would
entertain a wish that Montenegro might be preserved intact
and unchanged by civilization as a study of what mankind
has once been.

Anxious to see something of the condition of the refugees,
and, if possible, of Montenegrin preparation, I decided to
go to Grahovo, the chief place of the canton of the same
name north of Cettinje. There is a direct road, but the
Prince advised me, for greater facility and economy of time,
to go by way of the Bocche di Cattaro, the direct road being
so difficult; and for Montenegrins, indeed, the usual route
is to return to Cattaro and then by boat to Risano, whence
a good Austrian road leads to Dragal on the frontier, whence
a fair one continues to Grahovo. Leaving Risano by early
light, there is barely time to see what was to be seen at
Grahovo, say two to three hours, and get back by dark.
The route lies through Crivoscie, scene of disaster to the
Austrian arms in 1869; and even an eye without military
training can see enough to say it were no shame to the
best troops in the world to be defeated by bellicose peasants
with the country in their hands. The road winds along
slopes more awful and dizzy than those of the Cettinje road
even, and where, from its tortuousness, artillery is useless;
and bands of courageous men might stop all passage by

rolling stones down on the troops. The limestone rock is upheaved in vertical dykes, which are like interminable walls, each of which is difficult to climb for an unencumbered pedestrian;—making any movement, except by the road, impossible to men who cannot run and jump like goats, and who know the ground imperfectly. Sharp angles in the face of the mountains would suddenly expose the head of a column to the fire of any number of men at close quarters. My plan had been to return to Ragusa by way of Trebinje, but the road that way was still worse. From Grahovo to Trebinje the distance by map is about fifteen miles; but I was told that, for all, the easier way was to Risano, thence by boat again to Castel Nuovo, and thence *vià* Zubci, the direct road being very difficult even for the mountaineers.

We had a witness of the reality of the war early in the journey, in an old couple escaping from Herzegovina with what remained of their goods, and who had travelled from Lubimir, one hour beyond Trebinje, all the way on foot, carrying burdens which I should have been sorry to shoulder for a mile. They could not have been less than seventy years old; and, judging from the general appearance of old people here, I should say they were more likely to be eighty. Further on we met a whole family, loaded also with their remaining substance, the mother carrying her youngest in its cradle strapped on her back, all loaded except a little fellow of three, who skipped along the rocky road barefooted in great glee. The father had remained behind; the grandfather, too old to fight, accompanied the family to security. A few sheep and goats went ahead, their present sole sustenance. Next was a wounded Bocchése, just from Gatschko, where he had lost a couple of fingers in a recent fight, and taken his revenge by cutting off the head of the Turk—an Aga of that country, whose sword, heavily mounted with silver, pistols of the same richness, and jacket covered with buttons and ornaments of heavy silver, he wore. His horse and all it carried were plunder. He told us that Dervish Pasha, with seven battalions of regulars (the battalion, I heard from best Austrian authority, not ranging higher in force than about 400 to 450 men), with two or three battalions of irregulars, had succeeded in re-victualling Piva, the body of Christians (to whom the informant belonged) being only 300 strong, and unable to hold the ground. The local authorities at Grahovo informed me that a convoy of provisions was in a day or two expected from Ragusa, at Trebinje, and that a grand attack was to be made. This was the reason, probably, that the forces which were around Gatschko were so small.

From every side I gathered confirmation of the opinion, that the insurrection was not prepared by outside intrigues; that the committees did not expect it, and were unprepared for it—unprepared to aid it efficiently. The number of good rifles was small in comparison with that of insurgents, and I saw numbers who carried the old-fashioned *tufek*. They complained that they were unable to attack the Turks with effect, on account of their guns not having any range, so that they had to choose positions where the troops came to close quarters. Rifles were, however, slowly arriving, and it was clearly impossible, with the sympathy existing for the insurgents in the Slav population of Austria, to devise or carry out measures which should prevent the introduction of arms and munitions in Herzegovina; and any attempt to follow up such rigorously, would then have made incalculable trouble for the Government. Some people in the Bocche di

Cattaro were contributing as much as the sixth of their income to the support of the insurgents.

The Crivoscians again, who formed by much the largest foreign element in the insurrection, were not to be restrained by any governmental order; and with the greatest resolution so to do, the Austrian authorities could not have prevented them from crossing the frontier when they pleased. The Montenegrins at Grahovo spoke highly of the fighting capacity of the Crivoscian, but said that he was invariably a thief. The men of the lower Herzegovina again were honest; but though the first to rise, indifferently good insurgents. The value of a man as a fighter depends apparently on his geographical position—the nearer the Montenegrin frontier the better the man; and in the lower country, where the predominance of the Mussulman element has been more complete, the character of the people is correspondingly debased. The people of that section, to use the words of a Montenegrin official, "think of nothing but the stick of the Turk;" while with the Montenegrin, the Crivoscian, and their kindred mountaineers, courage is the dominant quality, and the highest ambition is to die fighting: so that they only say of a man that he has died when he dies a natural death; they say of a man who has been killed in battle that "he is missing," and his family regard the peaceful death as a proper cause for mourning—not that in battle.

We met on the road, or were overtaken by, a number of men going home with booty, or wounds, or returning to fight, and the number of men visible other than those was very small. The number of women and children was very considerable, however. The "political captain" of the village said that there were about 1,000 distributed among the houses, the church, and camping out; some having brought

their flocks, and some nothing but the rags on their backs.
He said that those who had their flocks received nothing
from the Government; but those who had nothing, had a
small allowance. He had that morning given out the last
provisions in store, and until something more came there
was nothing to give them, except the ungathered maize
in the fields. Others were continually arriving, and some
of the fighting men were engaged in hunting out and
bringing in, wandering individuals or families from the mountains of Herzegovina. Here, too, was a rude hospital, where
such of the insurgent wounded as were near the Montenegrin frontier were brought as to the nearest point of safety.

We went to see some of the refugees—for the most part
women, and in such a state of rags and misery that they
would not have been allowed to beg in the streets of London,
with two or three old men past the fighting age even for this
country. [We overtook one going to the war from Crivoscie,
who had forgotten whether he was seventy-five or seventy-six.]
My companion asked what made them leave home to come
here. They did not seem to have any definite idea, except
that it was to escape from the Turks. It was evidently a
general panic, usual in insurrections in the Turkish provinces. Long experience has taught the Christians that the
repression of an insurrection is always accompanied by
general and murderous barbarity; and that once fighting
begins, there is no safety for Christians, women or children,
any more than men, except in flight across the borders, or
into the inaccessible mountains. The whole of Turkish
history justifies the apprehension—the habit of the Turk
being to strike without distinction of persons or criminality.
When questioned as to their special grievances, they all said
the same thing—the Turks robbed them, took whatever

they wanted—their animals, what they had in their houses, and even their daughters when they took a fancy to them, and they never saw them any more. Into this grievance we inquired most particularly, because it will be found to be the true tide-mark of Turkish oppression. In some provinces taxes may be intolerable and justice unattainable, and yet the Mussulman will not venture to carry away the women. They all assured me, both women and men, that it was common, and they complained bitterly of their bishops, who, when their girls were carried away, showed no zeal to reclaim them. One tall, haggard old woman, about sixty, stood listening like a statue of misery, and the tears began flooding her eyes and running down her wrinkled cheeks, not a muscle moving, watching my friend who interpreted, until finally, with the recital of some kindred suffering, the stone melted, and she buried her face in her ragged robe and burst into violent weeping. She had no soul left of all her family. By one way or another she was alone. It was brutal to question her further. My own eyes had tears too near for me to speak without giving way. I turned away, not to betray myself, and walked to the high road. Down by the church, they said, was the great assemblage— would I go to see them? These were only the hungry ones who had come for the bread no one had to give them. No, I didn't care to see or know anything more; I could do nothing, not even if my pockets were full. So I went to see the wounded, in smoky cabins, lying on the ground, their wounds unwashed, in dirty bandages ; no water to spare here, for all that they had was brought a mile on women's backs, the long drought having dried up all running water, and cisterns being all exhausted ; no surgeon either, and all grave wounds these. Outside one young man with a ball through his foot was bargaining for a gun to go back to the war with. He showed me laughingly the pieces of bone he had taken from his foot, and which he kept carefully wrapped in paper, as if something talismanic were in them. We went to two or three houses, all alike, except that some of the patients had beds. I learnt at Risano with great pleasure that an Austrian surgeon was going up to Grahovo to attend to the wounded, and that the Government intended sending food for the refugees. We reached Risano late in the evening, taking the steamer thence for Castel Nuovo the next morning.

At Castel Nuovo was the depôt and direction of the insurrection, arsenals, and storehouses, and seat of the distributing committee. The little strip of territory belonging to Turkey, which here comes down to the sea, afforded the most important facilities to the insurgents, and to reach it from Castel Nuovo was only a half-hour's walk. Here volunteers, rifles, ammunition, provisions, &c. were landed *ad libitum*, as I had the evidence of my own eyes to prove, and the insurgents had the freedom of the frontier, coming and going in absolute freedom. No concealment was practised whatever in conducting any kind of military operations which circumstances permitted.

I found that sharp fighting had been going on in the neighbourhood of Zubci, and that my hope of visiting the insurgent camp *viâ* Trebinje, or *vice versa*, was vain, for no communication that way was practicable, as I had got no escort, and I was assured that the country was most unsafe, even with the best escort I could have obtained. Besides, the insurgents were in motion, nobody knew where, and I was again compelled to make a flank movement to find them. I had, however, an opportunity of examining the fortress and barrack of Sutorina, destroyed by the insurgents, and the destruction of which called down on the authors of it a great deal of denunciation. It seemed to me, however, a measure admissible in a military point of view, if it had been complete, as the building was really a strong fortress, unassailable by any means in the hands of the insurgents, if once occupied by a Turkish force. Besides, the Christians were in entire uncertainty whether the Austrian Government might not at any day have allowed troops to land at Sutorina, as they had at Klek, in which case their most available and natural source of supplies would be cut off. I was able also to visit the place near Sutorina where the cartridges were manufactured, and got here an indication of the disorder and want of common sense in the conduct of their affairs, which told its story even more clearly than the fact that the insurgents could not be depended on to obey orders when their fancy led them in another direction. These cartridges were made for the whole insurrectionary force; and as the men were armed in part with rifles and part with tufeks, &c., and the ammunition distributed indiscriminately, it was clear that one-half must be badly served in any event; but as the ball in the cartridge was made small enough to suit the smallest calibre, and round, or as near round as bad casting brings it, the consequence was that the much-valued rifles were used with round balls, half filling the bore, the extreme range of which would certainly not be above 200 yards, doing small damage at that. In fact, the members of the committees in general seemed to think that to keep up an insurrection, it is only necessary to get as many men together as possible, and send in bread, rifles, and ammunition, anyhow and anywhere, trusting to the chapter of accidents to keep things all right. The committees were badly organized; and though they contained men of unquestionable ability and devotion to the cause, there was not one man, so far as I saw, who had any conception of what insurrectionary organization ought to be. In fact, what I saw at Castel Nuovo alone would have been sufficient to assure me that there had been no preparation for insurrection, or definite purpose in direction.

This was the greatest weakness of the movement. There was no want of men—there were more than could be armed; nor is the want of military organization and discipline of great importance in a war where no regular operations are possible, and where, from the difficulty of the country, no great danger of surprises by the troops is to be apprehended. Even the question of provisions is one of less importance than in regular operations; and these men were accustomed to go two or three days without bread, and sometimes thirty-six hours without water; they rarely drink coffee, or even raki, in their movements, and are gay under privation which would paralyze any regular troops. But men who have not ammunition fit for their use, and are obliged to expose themselves to the fire of the Turkish breechloaders for a certain time before they can get near enough to do any harm in return, must have more than ordinary military courage to effect anything beyond closing difficult passes, and keeping the troops on the *qui vive*. To inflict any material damage on the regulars, they needed not only rifles, but ammunition for rifles, and this the committees had not had experience enough to understand the meaning of.

To see anything of the Turkish side of the question, it was necessary to get back to Ragusa, and to Ragusa I went by steamer again.

CHAPTER III.

DURING my absence in Cettinje the bands of the upper Herzegovina had come down and taken possession of the road to Trebinje, and had captured a provision train and carried it off to their camp at Glavski-dol. Hussein Pasha had sent out a battalion, with a strong squad of Mussulmans of Trebinje, to attack the camp, and they had been drawn by Peko Pawlovics into an ambush and utterly defeated, leaving eighty dead bodies behind them, amongst whom were several leading Beys of Trebinje, the main force escaping to the shelter of the block-houses in uncontrolled panic. The Pasha organized another expedition, which, however, after a slight skirmish on the main road, retreated to Trebinje again, and the insurgents held undisturbed possession of the road.

When I proposed to go to the beleaguered city there had been for several days no news, the foot postman being inter-dicted. But a Ragusa fiacre and an undaunted coachman were found equal to the occasion, and in company with correspondents of an American, a French, and an Italian journal, furnished with the Turkish visa, and with the in-surgents well warned that we were not enemies, I started. For three or four miles the road is either in Austrian territory or close to it, and protected by two blockhouses, Czarina

and Drien. This position is very wild, but, Drien once
passed, we had before us a drive of three hours, through a
country not nearly so difficult as any part of Montenegro
which I have seen, and found the whole country, with the
exception of the hills just about Drien on the frontier, and
three or four miles near Trebinje, entirely abandoned to the
insurgents. The guard over a store of flour, &c. on the
Austrian frontier, assured us that for five days not even the
post had passed over the space so given up. The outposts
were sufficiently on the *qui vive* to jnstify one in thinking
that the enemy had been sighted. Three Austrian peasants
from Brieno, waiting a chance to go to Trebinje, begged the
protection of our shadow, in abject fear of finding themselves
alone face to face with the terrible " Montenegrins."

Not a long rifle-shot from the outposts the driver pointed
out the locality of the beginning of the "great fight" where
the convoy was taken. The ground was still red with blood
in spots along the road, and the Brienesi assured us that
half an hour further on we should find the "Greeks." The
country gives capital cover, though not precipitous. It seems
from the hills at Drien to be a plain, but when we get down
into it we find it cut up by numerous shallow ravines, and
studded with crags and spurs of limestone from three to ten
feet high, between which, in the interstices, were rooted
scrubby oaks and other bushes. A thousand men might lie
within a hundred feet of the road and not show a cap. The
whole region was deserted by every living creature, so far as
we could see. Watching carefully, I saw finally, a short rifle-
shot from the road, a human head above a rock, but in a
moment it had disappeared. Half-way through this dreary
waste, which I can only compare to a vast glacier turned
into stone, where a wretched vegetation had found a myste-

rious *raison d'être*, the peasants pointed out to us a dead
Turkish soldier lying by the roadside, his face in the mud
left by the recent rain, divested of every article of clothing
but his shirt, but in no wise mutilated. He was a corporal,
we afterwards found, killed in the last skirmish, and had lain
there ever since, the troops not daring to venture so far to
recover the body.

We saw no other sign of humanity until, with our frantic
escort of Brienesi racing ahead of the carriage at its best
speed, we fell in with the outposts of the Turks not far from
Duzi, where a battalion had come out to protect the wood-
cutters. They were keeping a very lively look-out from every
little eminence, but asked us no questions.

Trebinje is a dull place to be blockaded in, and, as no
news had come from the outside world for five days, we were
much stared and wondered at. The surgeon of the Pasha met
us at the entrance of the city and led us to the Konak, where
his Excellency received us with all the politeness and gravity
of a true Turk, and gave us the official version of all the
recent affairs, in all of which he assured us, except the one
in which the convoy was taken, the troops had been victorious. In this he admitted that they had been drawn into
an ambuscade, and had some twenty or thirty men killed. I
did not say to him that a friend of mine visiting the insurgent
camp had counted eighty heads stuck up on poles, nor did I
ask why, if the insurgents had been so triumphantly scattered
in the last affair, according to his account of it, the troops
had not brought away their dead corporal. The poor fellow
was so amiable and courteous, and seemed so despondent
and so really unable to understand why the insurgents should
try to do them so much harm, that I had not the heart to
dispel the least of his illusions, but consoled him with the

assurance that diplomacy would soon settle the question.
He informed us that he had 2,000 troops, but that bands
of the insurgents, instigated by foreign emissaries, were
fomenting the movement and drawing the peaceable people
into it, overrunning the country and burning the villages of
those who refused to join them, so that it was impossible for
the troops to go from one place to another. It was evident
that he really believed this version of the whole matter, and
we left his faith undisturbed. His soldiers were evidently
not starving, but luxuries were not rife. We got some eggs,
a couple of boxes of sardines, and some bread and Dutch
cheese, and this was all, except half-dried grapes and sour
wine, that Trebinje could command.

The Pasha spoke a little French, and manifested some
acquaintance with European matters, asking, amongst other
things, how many people were employed on "The Times." I
replied, "a tabor" (battalion), knowing that a tabor meant,
with them, anything from one to eight hundred men. He
asked me if there were not other journals of great circulation
printed in London, and on my replying in the affirmative,
wondered why they did not consolidate and make one much
greater. He could not understand the value of an opposition. There was something really pathetic and touching
in his manner of regarding the persecution of the insurgents
and the grievance and uncomfortableness of his situation—
something accordant with the popular idea of oriental civilization: dreamy and poetical; intensely unpractical, at least.

The sole European official in the city, the Austrian Consular Agent, Vercevics, invited us to coffee, and welcomed us
with a cordiality which was in itself an expression of the
ennui of his position. He had been fourteen years there,
he said, and his heart was sickened more at what he saw the

unhappy Christians of the country suffer than from his solitude. The story he told fully confirms all I have said of the condition of the Rayah.

On one point I think his opinion valuable to the public, the more as he is, from his position, his years, and his constant relation with the common people and those with whom the casual traveller has no intercourse, and who only will tell their feelings to one they can thoroughly trust, a most competent witness in a matter on which people even here differ much—*i.e.* the probable fate of the Mussulman Slav population if the provinces fall into other hands. He said that the real antagonism is not so much between the Rayah and the Mussulman as between the Rayah and the Mussulman landlord, and that the mass of the Slav Mussulmans are poor, and indifferent to the distinctions which lie at the root of the difficulty with the Agas. There is, he said, a small number of fanatical Mahometans who will leave the country if it pass under Christian domination, and some of the old aristocracy who will fight hard against the change; but the mass will be better content under any Government which gives them justice than they are now without it, and will not be disturbed by any political change. Of this, he said, he could furnish strong confirmation if we had the time to look into his documents, but, as we had only a short time at our disposal, we were unable to do so. The difficulties, he said, of a solution of this question are much exaggerated by those interested in keeping up the *status quo*, but he was absolutely certain that for the great mass of the Mussulman population, almost as poor and oppressed as their Christian compatriots, the change would be a welcome one.

The troops were a good-looking set of fellows, cheerful, patient, and full of life and even frolic, but almost as ragged

as the insurgents, while as to the irregulars they were neither
better looking nor better armed. The Turkish regulars are
a fine body of men physically, but it seemed pitiful to send
them, with such organization and in such leading as they had,
to fight where nothing but perfect discipline can make head,
even if that could, and where every element of military
morale is requisite to secure solidity, not to speak of success.
In all cases where I have been amongst Turkish regulars I
have found my favourable personal impression confirmed.
Brutal and bloodthirsty they can be at times, when Christians
are concerned, but apart from this they seem docile, cheerful,
gay even. It seems to me that nothing can account for it,
except a total want of intellectual excitability, accompanied
with abundant animal life. As for Christians, they are always
accustomed to consider them as of less value than dumb
brutes, and generally a Turk will treat a dog with a tender-
ness as remarkable as his brutality towards a Christian. One
can only say that at heart he is a good fellow, and that his
religion is to blame.

Our return to Ragusa was made with as little incident as
our journey out. We found the next day that the rebel
sentries had taken account of us and sent in an accurate
description of the whole party.

The new arrivals of Turkish troops at Klek, and the
descent of the insurgent bands into Lower Herzegovina,
consequent on the decision of Montenegro not to enter into
the affair, led to an expedition to close the road from the sea
at Klek. Unfortunately for the plan, it was known to the
committees and their friends, and so, finally, to everybody,
including the watchful Turkish officials at Ragusa; and
when, after junction of the bands of Ljubibratics and Peko
with those of the Zubci, &c. they started for Klek, the Turkish

commanders were on the look-out with full knowledge of the insurgent plans, which were to take possession of Klek as a permanent position and make it the base of operations. Of the whole number of insurgents in the bands, about 2,000 were selected, and, by long, rapid marches, went from Glavski-dol through the Popovo plain, intending to attack Ljubinje, a strong Mussulman village, where were great quantities of supplies, to take possession of these, and carry them off to Klek to serve as provisionment for their camp.

At one of the Popovo villages where they stopped, they were informed that a large Turkish force was at Ljubinje, but nothing at Klek, where a convoy was to arrive next day, and the chief of the village, who gave the information, advised that the insurgents should not go to Ljubinje but to Klek, where there were no troops. Following the advice, they found at Utovu a body of troops coming from Klek holding the road in front of them, and had scarcely engaged them when they heard the trumpets of another column coming from Stolaz on their rear. A sharp attack by Peko's men on the right wing of the Turks drove them back and opened the way to the insurgents, who had barely cleared the hills on the Popovo side of the road when the first shots of the advancing troops from Stolaz fell amongst their rear harmlessly ; they lost four killed, and brought their wounded, seventeen, to Ragusa, They brought away fifty-eight noses of Turks killed, and as compensation for the treachery burned the village at which they had been falsely informed, on their way back.

Returning, the chiefs made their main station at Grebci, three hours from Ragusa and just across the frontier, convenient for supplies, and easily defensible from the Herzegovina side.

I decided to go up at once and spend a few days in the camp, but Ljubibratics coming into Ragusa with an attack of fever, I paid him a visit at the hotel, and received from him a summary of the general desires and aims of the un-political Herzegovinian, *i. e.* a partisan of none of the external combinations, but of the freedom, as far as might be, of the people of the province. Without attaching greater importance to him than is his due, I think he said what his compatriots really desired at that time, and which was more than would have pacified them a month earlier.

When I entered his room he was on the point of sending a message to me, and we at once entered on a discussion of Herzegovinian affairs and of public opinion in England in reference to the movement. He was strongly opposed to any foreign domination of the Slav organization, and especially to that of Russia; but he said that he and his compatriots were decided to put an end to Turkish misgovernment of their province, by driving out the Turk or leaving the country depopulated and ruined. They had tried before and had experience of Turkish promises and reforms, and now they were resolved to make the struggle conclusive : if they could not live free in their own country, free from this horrible system of slavery, which made the Herzegovinian nothing more than a brute, without instruction, without hopes, and without the commonest rights of humanity, they would drive their families out of the country and leave the Turk nothing but the bare and impoverished land—they would fight while they could hold together, and, when nothing more was possible, would divide into small parties and ravage and harry the Turks until they themselves were exterminated. In reply to what would content them in the way of concessions, he said, promptly: " From the Turk nothing less than autonomy ; we have had enough of their promises, and will listen to no more. We cannot live under Turkish administration." "But," said I, "if the Powers intervene and guarantee reforms, would you refuse them ?" "Certainly," he replied, "we would accept under the guarantee of the Powers, if all united in it, any reforms which assured us personal liberty and security, if the execution of them were intrusted to the Prince of Montenegro or some of the Christian Powers. The reforms must be radical, and we know that such will not be put in execution by the Turks."

The departure for the camp was postponed for one day longer, as there were consultations with the committee, &c. ; and it was finally two p.m. before Ljubibratics left Ragusa, and, going by way of Gravosa and the river of Ombla, we began our ascent of the mountain road, which, after passing through the narrow strip of Dalmatia which divides Herzegovina from the sea, leads into the valley of Grebci just across the frontier. As far as Ossoinics the road was fair, always steep, between bare, slippery rocks—two or three little villages on the way, with some level land with vineyards and olive-trees, but for the most part rugged declivities without other herbage than scanty and scrubby trees—getting more and more steep and broken as we approach the frontier, and finally so bad that it was like mounting a staircase with huge steps. We passed the frontier after sunset, and entered by the twilight into another of those huge broken amphitheatres of desolation of which I described one in Montenegro, down the slope of which we descended in the increasing obscurity, the light barely sufficing to show us the yawning clefts in the limestone-rock, among which the path led, zig-zag, here and there, between crags and sharp-cornered ledges, and when we reached the last declivity, and came in sight of the camp-fires, we found that it was barely possible to see where to put our feet. The pickets were going out for their guard of the passes, merry as children. Grebci is a fair type of the villages of the Herzegovinian hills, and a village of forty or fifty houses, mostly of one story, with the ground for floor, the walls of uncut stone, without mortar, and the roofs of stone or thatch, laid on small tree trunks, the whole most primitive and inexpensive. There are no chimneys, and the fire is made in the middle of the floor. Scarcely any glazed windows, but a hole in the wall, shut by a door when need is, plenty of holes in the roof for ventilation and escape of smoke. The night being bright and still, all the world was out-of-doors, every house having its squad of ten to twenty men, its separate camp-fire in the little garden or in the street. We found each fire surrounded by a circle of insurgents, all talking, laughing, and clamouring for the news as we came by.

We stopped for the moment at the Italian head-quarters, where the "*Squadra Italiana*" (sifted down from its original fifty or more of dubious material to a dozen resolute fellows, with one Frenchman, Barbieux[1]) were merrier and more musical than all the rest. Like the others, they were in wretched plight as to their externals. Their shoes were patched, of all constructions, most of them hardly keeping their feet from the rocks, and the rest of their equipment made up to correspond. The voivode spoke in the highest terms of their courage and endurance. They were, he said,

[1] One of the few foreigners who adhered to the movement throughout, dying at Grahovo of diphtheria in the Montenegrin campaign, just after the battle of Vucidol, a brave man, a good soldier, and a lover of human freedom. Those who knew him well will ever remember him with regret at the untimely end of his career.

the life of the camp, and greatly respected by the actual insurgents, whose great delight was to get round their quarters at night and listen to their songs. Near by theirs were the quarters of ten Russians, who had just joined— tough, solid-looking fellows; beyond these the Zubcians and the men of the confines of Montenegro. I might go on and make a catalogue like Homer's if I had a care. These were the picked and solid material of the force under Ljubibratics and Peko, about 900 men, to whom, under emergencies, were added several hundred more. Of these about 250 were Montenegrins, the rest mainly Herzegovinians. We were introduced to Peko; Melentie, the fighting Archimandrite of Duzi; Luka Petcovics and the popes Bogdan Simonics, Minja, and Milo. We were passed from hand to hand, and when salutations were over, went to a sort of granary, where assembly was held, and where, while we lay on a couch of straw spread on the ground, or sat on rude log seats, the Italians held their usual evening's entertainment, and while, at our backs, the half of a goat was roasting for our supper, we listened to the songs of many nations— French, Italian, Servian, Polish, with some of incomprehensible *patois* between.

When the meat was roasted it was laid on a heavy platform, which served for bedstead at night and table by day, and was hacked to pieces by the yataghans which had served at Utovu. It was late, and we were all tired, which, with other reasons needless to enumerate, made my appetite slight, and after supper the correspondents were called off, and, salutation made, we were shown our quarters, one of the upper rooms of the chief house of the village. There were two rooms on the story, and in the outer a huge fire was blazing in the middle of the tiled floor, which filled the place with blinding smoke. In the other was spread some fresh, clean straw, also on bare tiles, and here, as in the choicest quarters they could give us, we five lay down to sleep, the room hot and smoky; but, weary as we were with our four hours' hard and rapid climb, even the thin straw which allowed us to recognize the tiles too well, seemed a grateful bed. Scarcely, however, had we begun to doze when we were aware of invading armies more numerous and less easily repulsed than the Bashi-bazooks, who left no chance for sleep. If, in sheer exhaustion, I dozed for a moment after a successful chase, I was awakened by a sharp attack in another quarter. At length, in sheer desperation, I sat up, put my back to the wall, and lighted a cigar, abandoning all hope of repose.

Long before daybreak we got up, called our giant Herzegovinian keeper, and bade him make us some coffee. He blew the fire into a flame, and, as the good we desired was plentiful in camp—Peko having, the day before, captured a convoy of six mules loaded with coffee and sugar, on the Trebinje road—we had two cups each. By this time day had begun to break, and I walked out. The camp fires were still burning, and around every fire lay the squad it belonged to stretched on the bare ground in a sleep so sound that even our walking among them scarcely waked one. The clear October night was not tropical, and I found my overcoat necessary; but many of the insurgents had not even a blanket, and most of the Italians and all the Russians were sleeping under the stars.

I had intended to pass two or three days in camp, but found myself incapable of the degree of endurance required. The voivode went off to the council of war, and then to examine the condition of the squads who were to take part in a movement that day, and we strolled about till breakfast. We left at eight a.m., Ljubibratics walking with us part of the way to talk of the politics of the question. He is a man of education and of political knowledge, and understood the value of public opinion in England, and easily accepted what I said to him of the importance of moderating the demands of the insurgents to the standard of reasonable and practicable concession, if they wished England to interest herself in a favourable settlement of the affair. "If England interests herself in our condition, I have a hope that it may be bettered," were his last words.

CHAPTER IV.

S Ljubibratics appears to the public a principal figure in the record of this affair, and as in subsequent military matters he had little importance, I will at this point show what part was his in a movement the spontaneity of which has been so much denied. Native of a village near Trebinje, he in early life came to Dalmatia, where he is remembered as a shop-boy. When the affair of 1862, known as the insurrection of Luka Vukalovics, broke out, Ljubibratics (an assumed name; his real one I have forgotten) joined it, and was well spoken of for bravery.

A dreamer and enthusiast, with little practical knowledge of men and none of military matters, the part he took in the present insurrection was one of agitation, and as he spoke fluently both French and Italian, he drew round himself all the foreign volunteers, and by his hostility to all barbarous customs, and attempt to follow those of civilized warfare, he secured their adherence and a certain consideration beyond Herzegovina, while he alienated most of the mountaineers, who had no respect for those refinements. When energetic military operations began he found the most valuable fighting element deserting him, and he was left at Grebci with his volunteers and the men of the plain, who were better insurgents when no fighting was to be done than when the Turks were in sight. The mountaineers (Montenegrins, Banianici, Zubcians, Pivans, Crivoscians, &c.) had sufficient acumen to see that he was too irresolute and ideal to have any military success, and his proclamations and moral influence they had no use for. He played the part, *very* much in miniature, which Kossuth had in Hungary in 1849.

But this was not his real value to us. The part he took and the influence he exerted were greatest at the beginning of the outbreak, and his hostility to Russian, and even Montenegrin, influence in the insurrection, which finally led to his being driven out of the camp and Upper Herzegovina by Peko and the party which favoured Montenegro; as well as the control he had over the movement in its early phases, showed that he was, as he declared (and, whatever his faults, I have never doubted his entire honesty), and as I had other and sufficient later reasons for believing, no emissary of either Russia or Montenegro, and if of Servians, only of a party, or of individuals, and anxious that Herzegovina should be organized independently of any foreign influence.

He showed as little political sagacity as military talent; for he could not have failed to understand, with tolerable political good sense, that the only part of Herzegovina capable of resisting the Turk was exactly that which was, and must necessarily be, under the sole influence of Montenegro. But the facts, that he obeyed no instructions from Montenegro, and finally even threw off his Servian advisers; that he was always kept in the field through the efforts of the Zara committee, hostile *always* to Montenegro; that the moment the Montenegrins took control and direction of the movement he was driven out and compelled to go beyond the Narenta; and that with all this he was the most influential person connected with the revolution in this early phase, shows with sufficient conclusiveness that at least Russia had not then anything to do with the matter. The animosity of Ljubibratics to the Russian influence was as open as it was bitter, and of this I had ample evidence at all times.

In the lull which followed the defeat at Utovu, the incongruous elements of which Ljubibratics and Peko were representatives, broke into open dissension, each accusing the other of being the cause of the defeat, and Peko with all the Mountain, throwing off all respect for Ljubibratics's authority, and breaking up the camp at Grebci, went off to Zubci, and Ljubibratics followed, only controlling, however, a few reliable volunteers, the indifferent war material of Popovopolje, and a quantity of drift-wood, always at the distribution of bread, and never at a skirmish. General discouragement ensued. At this time there was great discord, and no power of resistance, except in the mountain country; and if the Turkish commanders had had any energy they would have followed up their advantages by occupying all the strategical points of the plain country, and by an effective movement on Zubci. Shefket Pasha, subsequently known better in Bulgaria, found it more to his taste to make military promenades and send despatches of victories where he had never even fought a battle; and the opportunity passed with two or three unimportant skirmishes, and the wanton devastation of the Popovo plain, at which, and the massacre which accompanied it, Shefket officiated in command of the column. By this act of barbarity five thousand refugees who had, on the guarantee of the Imperial Commissioner at Mostar, gone back to their homes, accepted the protection of the Porte and resumed the tillage of their fields, were driven back in wild panic across the Dalmatian frontier, all the men of the villages who fell into the hands of the troops, being either

:illed or taken prisoners to Trebinje, the rest, with the
vomen and children, escaping to Austrian territory, leaving
)ehind them their effects, which were pillaged and carried off
)y the troop and Bashi-bazooks, who also defiled and ruined
ill the churches. This characteristic treatment of the first
;ection of the country which had accepted the pacification
)f course made further attempts to induce the Christians to
eturn, useless. The Turkish army showed the least possible
nclination to pacific conduct, and very little to active
iostilities. The whole country was kept in panic by in-
lividual cases of barbarity and murder, but no military
:fficiency helped to an issue. They would accept no peace
ind could make no war. The Christians who had not joined
he revolt were, from the beginning, robbed, beaten, often
:illed, numerous cases of such murders coming to my
:nowledge, some by personal investigation : the consular
Commission finding, at the early date of their journey, dead
)odies by the road-side where they travelled, which the
roops would not even bury or permit the Christians to
)ury, and on one occasion when the consuls had made a
endezvous with a body of insurgents, the authorities sent a
)ody of troops to attack the Christians, under circumstances
vhich satisfied the Commission that the intention of the
?asha was to compromise them and provoke the insurgents
o attack them, or to catch the latter thrown off their guard
)y the consular visit, and capture or kill them. Herze-
;ovina was an infernal chaos. Neither Turk nor Christian
howed any evidence of organization or control. The Aus-
rian committees sent aid in a limited and irregular way, but
he people at large took a faint-hearted part in the wars,
ind a concession which would have secured simply personal
ecurity, and justice before the tribunals, would have left the

agitators in hopeless isolation. Servia and Montenegro had failed them, and no hope was held out. Diplomacy, if it ever did any good might have been expected to do so here. But it failed, as it always fails, because it finds in humanity only a kind of chessmen, and thinks that it can control them as though there were no flesh and blood—no passion or ambition, but that they must move by order like automata. It regards the fictions of its own creation as realities, and expects a treaty to control those whom not even their own interest will always control, like children who draw a line in the sand, and agree not to pass it, and if a bold one defies the fiction, the game is broken up, and nobody knows what to do next. It is only when the diplomat has the sword girt on, that he has any vital existence for irrational organizations like the Porte.

The Popovo affair showed not only a new opportunity lost, but a radical incapacity in the organization of the Ottoman Government to employ an opportunity for retrieving the blunders which its local administrators might make. The return of the people of Popovo was an important event, and one which the Porte felt the full importance of, as was shown by the congratulatory despatches exchanged on the subject. The Turks had only to keep away from the district to secure the full effect of the new adhesion to their *promised* reforms, but even this they were incapable of. Shefket Pasha must in some way show the solicitude of the Porte over its returning children, and his military promenade showed that neither reform nor justice was possible. The elements on which his authority and that of his government rested were utterly uncontrollable, and opportunity was irresistible—violence was the natural state.

What was particularly instructive in this affair was that

the Popovo villages, though long time deserted by the majority of their proper inhabitants, had not been pillaged or otherwise molested, with the exception of one which was burned by Ljubibratics after **Utovu, as** described. The Christian insurgents had passed by them, and left them un-disturbed, and the Bashi-bazooks of **Trebinje or** Stolatz had never dared come so far without the protection of the regulars. As soon, therefore, as a **regular** force went, the Bashi-bazooks made their opportunity, and, unchecked by the disciplined forces, or their officers, did what pleased them. And flagrant as was the case, and strong as were the reclamations, no notice was ever taken of the authors of the outrage, or punishment inflicted on the responsible in-dividuals. **Some time after, Shefket was sent away in dis-grace for** being **defeated, and** went to Bulgaria to repeat on a larger scale the experiment of **Popovo.** The massacre took place October 14th, and on the strength of my repre-sentations to Mr. Holmes at Mostar, the consul-general of the Porte at Ragusa was ordered to make an inquiry, which he did, and he reported confirming my statements, when his re-port was rejected by the government at Constantinople, and Constant Pasha was ordered to make a new inquiry, which he did in the most convenient manner, and with the most satisfactory results. He paid no attention to the evidence, and reported that the outrage had never occurred. From such seed what could be expected but the harvest of Batok and Phillipopolis? A reference to the blue book will show the efficacy of diplomatic interference.[1] Shefket is

---

[1] SIR H. ELLIOT TO THE EARL OF DERBY.

My Lord,   *Therapia, November,* 23, 1875.

I directed Mr. Sandison to remark to the Porte that, although a con-siderable time had elapsed since the report had been received of the massacre at Popovopolje of a number of the Christian refugees who had

always equal to the opportunity, **and when Constant is not
at hand Edib Effendi** will do quite as well.   The **system is,
has been, and will be** while it exists, the same; for its
foundation   is   a   democracy   of   ignorance,   fanaticism,
sensuality, and brutality.

returned to their homes, we had not heard of any one having been
punished for the outrage.

Mr. Sandison having to-day spoken in this sense to the Grand **Vizier,
His** Highness at once telegraphed to the Governor-General of Bosnia to
inquire what had been done to insure the punishment of those concerned
in the murders.

I have, &c.,

(Signed)   HENRY ELLIOT.

CHAPTER V.

THERE being a complete lull in military operations, I determined to see what was passing at
the Turkish head-quarters, and in company with
the correspondent of "Le Temps" and a Belgian engineer
returning to his road-making between Mostar and Seraievo,
I went to Mostar.

The journey by diligence from Ragusa to Metkovich is
one which has a twofold interest. The tourist finds a succession of enchanting views, passages of rare picturesque
material, little nooks of sea-coast, with fringes of plain, where
the olive and vine flourish, and the palm puts forward a
claim to naturalization, if not to utility; jutting crags of
rock, headlands of massive limestone, where, with a good
south-west wind blowing, the marine painter would find his
best themes before him; an alternation of garden and desert
and sea; the Adriatic, with its many islands on the one
side, and the grey, bare range of mountains which forms the
boundary between Dalmatia and European Turkey, full of
exquisite hues and tints, on the other, and the road following all the sinuosities of the coast, making a whole of an
attractiveness I have never seen surpassed.

But the economist can only be reminded that this range
of barren mountain is merely the fringe of a great fertile

country inland, and that these bays and ports, with which
the coast is favoured, are the natural outlets of that country;
that along the crest of that ridge runs the boundary between
two empires, and that in this division, the result of mere
political chances, lies the secret of the poverty of both
countries : Dalmatia, with all its marvellous maritime facilities on one side, without a country to open into or give
egress to ; and Bosnia and Herzegovina, with all their interests, shut out of the world of commerce for want of the
commercial enterprise which languishes on the other side of
the line.   I have often thought of the economical absurdity
of this situation, but never realized it so well as when winding in and out from early dawn till evening on this post-
road, and thinking that if the Austrians could only make the
post-road on the other side of the mountains, we should
have made the distance on it in less than half the time, and
that it would become a great highway of commerce and
travel.   These two artificially separated provinces are lan-
guishing, impoverished, for want of union under one Government, which can make roads and develop in tranquillity the
resources which are now idle in the earth, as well as lift
into comparative comfort and prosperity a people ground
down in a misery and poverty which has no adequate comparison in our English experience.

The knowledge of this necessity is one of the most vivid
impressions in the minds of the Slav population on both
sides of the frontier, and supplies one of the most powerful
elements in that tendency to agitation for the freedom of
Bosnia, &c., in the Dalmatian population.

We had to pass the strip of Turkish country at Klek, and
here had another occasion to see the administrative incompetence of Turkish officials.   The road is a good one on

both sides of this territory, but here falls off into indifference; and at one part we were obliged to get out and walk up a long steep hill, while the diligence was drawn up by half-a-dozen oxen, being absolutely impracticable to the horses, simply because the Porte, in its mere suspicion or intolerance of any change, or of any foreign interference, forbade a slight change in the road, which would have made the grade easy. At Klek we saw the usual battalion encamped, the few steamers in the narrow bay, and the desolation of Herzegovina, every house by the road being burnt. We were told that 2,000 troops had gone up the day before, but all figures in this country have only comparative meaning, and are by no means to be taken as the expression of a definite idea.

Metkovich is a wretched little place, which might be a flourishing port if there were not a Turkish custom-house a rifle-shot above it on the Narenta, and a Turkish administration beyond. Below it the Narenta widens out into enormous marshes, and loses much of its character as a river; but when the projected dyking, deepening, and draining are accomplished, the marsh will be a fertile plain, and the Narenta navigable for considerable vessels up to Metkovich. It is navigable now for schooners, but there seems to be little trade. Here we made a bargain with an araba to take us to Mostar (nine hours); and your readers who know what it is to be jolted in a farm cart over a road, rocky or paved with unassorted pebbles, without being able to get refreshment of any kind on the way, can imagine the pleasure we found in these hours, of which at least seven were passed in a country without the slightest picturesque interest, every village by the way, except one Turkish, being burnt or demolished, or both; scowling Bashi-bazooks along the way in the hungry temper of mid-Ramadan, and we the only Christians in sight. Among these irregulars were boys of twelve and fourteen years of age, with *tufek* and pistols, and all the swagger of incipient brigands. We had a large tract of forest to pass through, here and there a little tract being under a semi-cultivation. The body of a dead Christian lay by the roadside, covered over with stones and boughs ; and the engineer pointed out to us by the roadside a Mussulman, who kept a raki shop near by, who had a few weeks before deliberately butchered and decapitated before his eyes a Christian engaged in cultivating his maize field, not a word having passed between the murderer and his victim previous to the attack. The engineer made a complaint to the authorities, and the Mussulman was put in prison for three days !

Descending the long slope into the valley, at the upper entrance of which, in a gorge where the Narenta passes, is Mostar, the whole character of the landscape changes, and we come on a fertile plain where war has left no trace, and where vineyards and olive orchards reappear. Surrounded on all sides by mountains, grey and bare as those of the other parts of the province, with running streams fringed with trees, the grand lines of mountain sweeping away and bending down to the pass where the city lies, with its minarets thin and white, the valley seemed like an oasis of Italy in the wilderness of grey rock. I don't remember a city among all I have ever seen so completely pictorial as Mostar. The mountains close in on it, and the rapid Narenta rushes eddying through the gorge on both sides of which the city lies, and both above and below lies a plain, circled by mountains, the upper one (which we only see after having entered the city and climbed up the heights on which it rises) being still more luxuriant, fertile, and picturesque even than the lower, through which we had passed. Numerous mosques add to the beauty of its external *ensemble*, and over the river is a high, single-arched bridge, dating back from centuries before the Turks came in. Tower and gateway, jalousies and bazaars, dirty and narrow streets crowded with soldiers and officers, pack-horses and Bashibazooks, fez and turban—what every Turkish town is in effect, Mostar is, but poor and shabby inside as beautiful and pictorial from without. The houses are all mean and small, the bazaars filled with trashy and Brummagem wares, and it was impossible not to be disappointed and disgusted with the contrast between the outside and inside of the city.

The khans are as poor and dirty as can be, and we only found lodgings on the ground-floor of the principal one, in a room ordinarily devoted to the stable boys, with mattresses spread on the ground, which for our special use and luxury were covered first with an old dirty carpet. Remembering my experience in the insurgent camp, I had brought with me a supply of insect powder—fortunate prevision !—for, before I had even retired, I was in a worse condition than *chez* Ljubibratics.

I had been told before leaving Ragusa, by a recent arrival from Mostar, that there was great irritation among the population, and report was, for once, not in the least exaggerated. Scowling faces were common, and in more than one, undisguised malediction was visible, and by more than one mouth spoken, as the new Ghiaours edged their way through the crowd to the consul's quarters. We found Mr. Holmes and Signor Durando in rooms in the Casino—a sort of hotel—dirtier, if possible, than the khan, but a sort of European

formality and ugliness, which was not to be compared with
the picturesque filthiness of the khan.

Five minutes satisfied me that there was nothing to be
learnt in Mostar about anything but Turkish incompetence
and mendacity. The reports the consul had of affairs in
the interior were the "Arabian Nights," compared with the
exaggerations of Ragusa and the Slav press. We learnt on
the most solemn assurance of Server Pasha, that at the time
when we were with the insurgent chiefs in quiet, if not comfort, at or near the Dalmatian frontier, the same were being
beaten near Zubci, "*à plat couture*," with a loss of 160 killed
and many wounded.[1] I fortunately knew the exact location
of the corps of Ljubibratics, and that when this attack was
said to be made, there could not have been a hundred
insurgents at Zubci, and I had as positive and trustworthy
intelligence as any one can get, that there was no fight at all
at that time, only a few random shots being fired by the
small guard left there. But worse than this were the fables
concocted about battles at points which cannot be identified,
with corps of insurgents which never existed.

Of the affair at Popovo Server Pasha had not heard a
word, or, at least, declared that he had not, and, moreover,
that he could not believe a word of the report we brought,
and no member of the Commission had heard anything of

[1] I had informed your Highness on the 25th instant that, according
to a telegram from the Consulate-General at Ragusa, General Shevket
Pasha had arrived at Trebinje, and had achieved a success over the
rebels. It appears from a letter of the said General that, by clever
strategy, over 2,000 insurgents have been surrounded by the Imperial
troops at Grap (Grab), in the neighbourhood of Ojanpitcha (?) and completely routed. The insurgents were compelled to fly and to enter
Montenegro, leaving 160 dead on the field of battle.—*Server Pasha to
the Grand Vizier.*

it until our arrival ; the Pasha, on the contrary, having assured them that the people of Popovo had returned to their homes, and that troops had been sent to protect them from the insurgents, and this, eight days after the exodus of the Popovites !

In fact, several of the consuls assured me that Mostar was the worst place in the Herzegovina, or vicinity, to learn what was going on in the interior, and that for all they knew they were dependent on Ragusa ; that though there might be much exaggeration in the reports from insurgent sources, they were not, at least, sheer fabrications, like those sent to Constantinople to keep the Sultan content and the Pashas in their places. It did not take me two days, indeed, to see that the Turkish administrators there and in Constantinople alike were lapped in a fool's Elysium, seeing and believing what was agreeable, and that, in fact, almost nothing was being done towards the real work of repressing the insurrection. Troops were sent on to the interior, and accumulated in masses at the most convenient points ; but there appeared to be no man in the least capable of efficient military operations, and the only ones attempted were the revictualling of the forts. To send twenty wounded men from Gatchko to Stolatz required the escort of two battalions, and nothing moved without strong escort.

The number of troops was uncertain, doubtless not known by the authorities even, but estimated at the highest at forty battalions. One of the officials, who had kept as careful note as possible of the arrivals, said that there were thirty-three, and that in one battalion which he took the trouble to count there were barely 200 men, as they set out for the interior. There were already 2,000 in the hospitals, with an immense camp on the edge of the marshes of the Narenta, and in the higher country nothing but tents for the mass of the troops to live in, nearly all the houses being destroyed in the line from Mostar to the Baniani mountains.

Of the condition of the beasts of burden, what I had heard at Ragusa was not in the least exaggerated The supply of horses was running short, and it became difficult to get them for common use. All those of the neighbouring districts had been used up, or were in service, and the fine Hungarian ones imported *via* Klek broke down rapidly. The number of horses dead already was estimated at 3,000; and the most exhausting service was required to keep up the supplies of food for the troops. The rations were only meat and flour, with no facilities for baking the flour, and the supplies of firewood in some sections were very precarious. In the higher regions the snow was half-knee deep, and the condition of the battalions crowded into Gatschko, Stolatz, and other interior stations, with very limited accommodation, not to speak of those camped out in intervening stations, where the whole force must be under canvas, can be imagined when I say, on authority unquestionable and most friendly to the Porte, that the apathy which reigned over the soldiers was so complete, that no movements were made for days together, and that the men were in rags, and wretchedly provided with every necessary for comfort. As to the rags, I needed no evidence but that of my eyes; and as to the condition of the provision trains which passed through Mostar, I can say, without exaggeration, that there was not a horse in some of them that the Society for Prevention of Cruelty to Animals would allow to go in harness in the streets of London. There was neither hay nor barley left; and the supply of food on hand was always so small, that when at one time the insurgents stopped the way from Klek for two or three days, the Government was obliged to make requisition on private stores in Mostar, and all such were searched out thoroughly.

Add to this that the administrative condition of the city approached the chaotic, that no Christian went out at night, and the streets were left to the bands of native Mussulmans, who patrolled the town in these nights of Ramazan with unrestrained liberty to do what they pleased, and the authorities took no notice, even on the complaint of the consuls, of any barbarities they committed; that outside of the city there was no plan in operations, and no appearance of general direction; that no one in command knew anything about the country, and that the troops were extremely disheartened, and only desired to be let alone by the insurgents; that nobody in the Government knew what was passing anywhere else, and most of the officials believed that the insurrection was near its end, and that the Imperial and responsible Commissioner himself was possibly the worst informed of the whole, and you have the sum of what was to be known in Mostar.

The members of the Consular Commission were unanimous in the opinion that the Government was absolutely incompetent to meet the emergency, and that the only possible solution was a foreign military occupation of the country until order should be restored and the entire native population disarmed. From this opinion there was only one dissentient in the Commission—the representative of Austria—who held that though the only certain solution was that above indicated, there was another possible if the Porte would accept it, and which he was preparing to submit to the Commission and the Governments.

But the proposed change was an operation unprecedented

in the annals of Ottoman reform, and as the last word of
the Austrian representative, anxious to avert a catastrophe,
and enjoying a reputation second to none of his colleagues
for familiarity with the subject, it was to my mind a more
convincing argument against Turkish reform than if the
author had accepted simply the general judgment of the
Commission.

Herr Wassics hoped to avoid the necessity of a foreign
occupation of Bosnia and Herzegovina, and for this purpose
he proposed the convocation of an Assembly consisting of
representatives of the populations of those provinces, Christians and Mussulmans, who should themselves consult and
decide on their own future condition and the reforms to be
extended to the country.   But this would be simply amputa-
tion behind the ears.   It first proposed to deprive the Porte
of the initiative in the reforms to be granted, and then deprive the Mussulman population of its supremacy, and even
of any kind of superiority over the Christian ; would compel
the Turk to lay down the yataghan and take up the latest
weapons of civilization and progress, in order to maintain
even his equality with the infidel—the dog on whom he is
accustomed to wipe his feet; to save himself from being
voted out of legal existence by abdicating every privilege of
tradition, and that social and political superiority which
alone have enabled him to exist in the land.   Whatever
modifications of this general conclusion might be effected,
either in the way of recognizing minorities or protecting
vested interests, its execution struck me as equally difficult
with any other proposed.   It certainly would be less likely
to succeed and more troublesome to apply than occupation
pure and simple.   It is a remedy which, whatever diplomatic
pressure might bring the Porte to say of it, the wealthy and

privileged classes of the Mussulman population would only accept, under strong compulsion, and which no force, except an armed foreign one, could guarantee the operation of.

It seems to me, however, worth recording here as an indication of the exhaustion of all the means of conciliation, in the opinion of the people best acquainted with the country, even at that early period of the struggle, and a justification for the radical policy of reforming *from the outside* the Ottoman administration.

I called at the earliest available moment on Server Pasha, whom I had known in Crete, and from whom I had, in common with European public opinion, hoped much. He had the repute of being one of the most intelligent and liberal of Turkish functionaries. I found him in real or assumed ignorance of the actual condition of matters, and persuaded that the reforms he projected would effectually remove the dangers of the future. To him there was no more an insurrection, and all that remained to be done was to induce the people to return. Old acquaintance justified me in attempting to undeceive him on the former point, and though I could not flatter myself that he would admit, even if he believed, the statements I made to him concerning it— at any rate, he expressed himself freely and at length on the plans and hopes he entertained, without denying the difficulties of the case.

The measures he proposed were, firstly, the reformation of the Councils in such a way as to secure proper representation of the Christian interests, with a publication of the Civil Code in Slav and Turkish, as well as of the laws on the election of the members of the Councils, so that the population may clearly understand its rights ; modification of the regulation of the service to be rendered by the people

in making and repairing the roads, so that none shall be
obliged to work out of the districts in which they live; the
sentences of the courts to be published in both languages,
and signed in both by all the members; formation of a corps
of secret inspectors of all administrative details, the names of
these to be known only to the Government at Constantinople and the Governor-General; suppression of the existing
system of conscription of horses—all such service to be rendered on terms of compensation to be agreed upon by the
parties concerned; transformation of the tithes into land-
tax;[1] formation of a corps of Christian and Mussulman
inspectors and collectors of taxes; obligation both for proprietor and tenant to have all leases written and to submit
them to official registry ; and finally, reorganization of the

---

[1] ACTING CONSUL FREEMAN TO THE EARL OF DERBY.

My Lord, *Bosna Seraï, May* 26, 1876.

I have the honour to inform your Lordship that new arrangements
had latterly been made for the collection of the "Aashr," or tithe on
agricultural produce. The system of farming the tithe was entirely
abolished, and officials styled "Aashr Mudiri" had been appointed in
all the sandjaks, at a salary of 2,500 piastres a month each, with a considerable staff of subordinates to assess and collect the tax. Instructions, however, were received yesterday by telegraph from Constantinople to annul this arrangement, and it was publicly announced in the
"Idareh Medjliss," or Administrative Council, that the tithes would be
immediately offered for sale at public auction as heretofore. This will
undoubtedly produce a very bad impression in the country.

The Commission of Control continues to hold its sittings daily, but
its labours have as yet borne no fruits.

No decision has yet been come to as regards the "Bedel-i-Askerieh," or
tax in lieu of military service, although much time has been spent in
discussing the matter. It was announced that the tax was only to be
paid between the ages of 20 and 40, but the Government persists in
demanding the same gross amount as heretofore, and it is naturally
rather difficult to reconcile such conflicting instructions.

I have, &c.,

(Signed) EDWD. B. FREEMAN.

police, which is to be composed of both Christian and
Mussulman zapties. Most of these, he assured me, are in
course of execution. Yet I venture to say that to this day
Herzegovina has not realized the slightest practical benefit
from all his plans and labours. *Non possumus* is in the water-
mark of every Turkish edict of reform, no matter who the
Sultan, or who his Grand Vizier. The abolition of the conscription of horses was the first measure attacked : the Aga
was summoned to furnish them instead of the peasants, and
he took the first he could lay his hands on—the horses were
the same, and the pay.

In fact, the illustrations of the working under Server
Pasha's own eyes were very curious. The local medjlis was,
after nominal promulgation of the above reforms, called on
to sign a memorial to the Porte praising and endorsing the
administration of the province. The Christian members
were presented the memorial, written in Turkish, which
none of them could read, for signature, with the assurance
that it was in reference to the administration of the hospitals; but, versed in Turkish wiles, they took it to be
translated, and declined signing when they found out what
it was. *They were immediately dismissed from the Medjlis.
So much for independence of councils.*

I made the acquaintance of an army surgeon who had
been attending a Christian boy of thirteen, wantonly shot in
broad daylight by a Mussulman boy of twelve. The young
assassin was carried in triumph around the neighbourhood
by his comrades, and the wounded youth to the hospital. It
seemed that the young Turk had had a present of a rifle
(army pattern), and had gone out to try it. Seeing the
Christian lad gathering grapes in his mother's vineyard, he
took deliberate aim, and shot him through the body at close

quarters. He was a long time in a very critical state, but finally recovered, the family being obliged to pay all the expenses of his illness. I had all the particulars from the surgeon, and the facts as to investigation from the consuls, on whose complaint an investigation by the Turkish officials was ordered ; a report, fully recognizing the facts, was made, and there the affair ended. " Making a report " is, to the Turkish mind, the *ne plus ultra* of judicial investigation into any matter in which Mussulman deeds are called into question. The Pasha was astounded when the consuls protested against this trivial manner of treating the incident,. and replied, "Have we not made a report?" The culprit never was molested. The Turks divide their judicial proceedings in a manner ingenious, if not just ; they investigate Mussulman offences without any punishment, and punish the Christian without any investigation.

Nor is it only the Christian who receives injustice. Mussulmans who are lax in their duty share in the treatment due to the Christian. Of this I had a striking instance in the case of Avd Aga Biscevics, which proves that a liberal Mussulman may just as well be a Christian. The story in brief is as follows :—

A certain Christian of Mostar, one Tripacuics, being a man of influence, and in the way of certain Moslem interests, the Chaoush (non-commissioned officer of Zaptiehs), Osman Deinics, a chief of the fanatical Mussulman party, was employed to kill him, which he did. The family of Tripacuics demanding justice on the murderer, and witnesses testifying that it was the Chaoush Deinics, the Mussulman authorities declined to entertain the complaint, and subsequently one Georgio Civics, a relative of Tripacuics, took up the case so importunately that the parties interested

determined to get rid of him, and for this purpose they sent
to the inn which he kept a professed bravo, by the name
of Pivodics, a Mussulman, in company with another Mussulman, Melencics Jussuf. The two desired beds, but the inn
being full, they were refused, and so contented themselves
with drinking in company with several others already in the
guest-room, among whom was Biscevics. After that night
Pivodics was seen no more in Mostar, but was seen by many
next day in Metkovics, whence he went to Ragusa, where
also he was seen by acquaintances, and whence he went to
Constantinople. His family demanding him at the hand of
justice, Melencics Jussuf deposed that he was last seen at
the inn of Civics in company with certain other people, who
were all summoned as witnesses, but who all testified that
he left the inn in good health, and these were thrown into
prison till they should be willing to testify conformably.
Among them, of course, was Biscevics, who, although a
Mussulman, was equally refractory, and from that day, three
years before, the honest fellow had lain in prison (except at
intervals when he was brought out to testify in the case,
and, refusing to give false witness, was remanded again),
until Bairam of the third year, 1875, when, according to a
Mussulman usage, he was released on security, and after
twenty days' liberty in Mostar he escaped with the aid of
two Christians and came to Ragusa, not long after my
return from Mostar. He was a captain of the Reserves, and
besides imprisonment was degraded, and was anxious to get
a rifle to join the insurgents, and to let the whole world
know what justice is at Mostar. I may say that Aga Biscevics was in haste to get to Cettinje, as the only place of
perfect security and justice; and when I assured him he
was as safe in Ragusa as I was, he kissed the skirts of my

coat in raptures of gratitude and joy. He had not dared
to show himself for fear of being captured and carried back
to Mostar.

Now, a curious feature in the case, which illustrates the
value of Turkish reform and Turkish sincerity in the execution of them, at the moment when everything was being done
that the Porte *could do* to satisfy Europe of its capacity to
render justice to its Christian subjects, is this: Civics had
been taken out of prison to be tried by the newly organized
mixed council, by which Server Pasha was to show how
well things could be done in Mostar, and as the case was
clearly one of unjust imprisonment, he was acquitted; but
as the council subsequently was found to derange the course
in which justice was in the habit of running, it was soon
dissolved, and then Civics was rearrested, tried by the Kadi,
and sentenced to five years' imprisonment, and was still in
prison when I took down from the lips of the hero, Avd
Aga Biscevics, the above details, the case itself having been
briefly related to me by one of the consuls in Mostar.

CHAPTER VI.

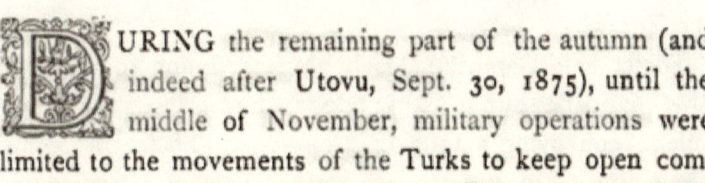URING the remaining part of the autumn (and indeed after Utovu, Sept. 30, 1875), until the middle of November, military operations were limited to the movements of the Turks to keep open communication with the various fortresses in the mountain country about Piva, Niksics, &c. The insurrection was without head or general direction from any side. The chief of Piva, Lazar Socica, had since the outbreak distinguished himself above all his fellow captains by the energy and daring of his raids, his attacks on the blockhouses distributed through the mountain country, and the exceptional discipline he obtained in his corps. Of the line of works which protected the road from the plain of Gatschko to the valley of the Tara he had destroyed all except that of Goransko, which was defended by artillery. In this campaign he used various devices, the most successful of which was a portable blockhouse, borne by the men, and which being thick enough to prevent the rifle-balls from penetrating, was carried up to the walls, where a mine under the the foundation was the means, generally, of bringing the garrison to surrender. Socica distinguished himself by his humanity as well as by his bravery, all the troops who sur-

rendered being conveyed in safety to the nearest fortress, and the barbarous practice of cutting off heads being entirely prevented in his command for a long time, and only finally given way to, owing to the fury excited in his men by the Turks exhuming some of the Christians killed in a skirmish and buried by their comrades, and decapitating the dead bodies. " After that," said Socica to me long subsequently, " I could not prevent my men from cutting off the heads of the Turks."

Socica held Garansko closely blockaded, and to relieve it Shefket Pasha set out with 3,000 regulars, artillery, and irregulars, convoying a train of provisions. Socica made his arrangements to oppose him at the Pass of Muratovizza, and sent to the chiefs of Baniani, Rudini, Zubci, &c., to ask them to unite in the defence. The number of insurgents collected was about 1,500, not much more than half of whom were present when the fight began. The road that leads through the Pass of Muratovizza is flanked on the left by three hills, more or less conical and abrupt, and on the right by a long, not precipitous, mountain slope with tolerable cover of boulders and forest. On the latter the insurgents were posted to await the entry of the troops. The first day, the attack of the insurgents was made as the Turks entered the pass, and resulted in stopping them, when they withdrew and waited till the following morning, the insurgents gathering, in the meanwhile, in greater force every hour. When the troops, on the second day, had entered the ravine, they were attacked along the whole line simultaneously, and took up positions on the conical hills, throwing up stone breast-works for protection, the Pasha on the central hill in the ruins of an old Palanka (one of the larger class of blockhouses), and the centre round them, the van and rear-guards on the hills at either end of the pass. The Pasha, finding the passage impossible, sent the artillery and what besides was saved, to the rear under cover of the hills, unobserved, during the fusillade, the insurgents having neglected to close the defile behind him, and in the course of the day and night managed to save the bulk of his army, the positions of the centre and vanguard being carried by assault by the insurgents. The position of the rear-guard was maintained through the night, the Pasha having told them to hold on to the last and he would go to attack the insurgents in the rear. The unfortunate rear-guard was entirely cut off, all but 100, who surrendered, being killed in the assault at daylight next morning. The pursuit of the Turkish main body was kept up to Gatschko by the bands which were arriving from more distant sections, and who were not in time to take part in the main battle. The total loss of the Turks in killed was 760, and 900 wounded, most of whom, as I learned later from the Turkish surgeons, died of want of care and hospital accommodation, there being no fuel obtainable without constant fighting, and the men having to remain in tents, with deep snow on the ground.

The loss of the Christians was 57 killed and 96 wounded, amongst the former being Vulé Agics, one of the most promising and bravest of the chiefs, the lieutenant of Socica, treacherously shot while negotiating for the surrender of a body of Turks who were surrounded.

This splendid victory revived immensely the courage of the Christians, while the arms and ammunition captured armed more and armed them better. Raouf Pasha, who had replaced the fussy Achmet Hamdi in command in Herzegovina, made a strong effort to restore the morale of the army and Turkish population, and collected as rapidly as possible a new and imposing force to relieve, not only Goransko but Niksics, which was now in great straits. He collected all the disposable troops from Mostar, and beyond, even, and called for reinforcements from Sienitza. The Turkish generals made loud accusations of violations of neutrality against Montenegro, and orders were sent from Constantinople to cross the frontier and attack the principality if the aid to the insurgents was maintained, and as the insurrection was (and is still) supposed by many to be merely the work of the Montenegrins, I determined to go into Montenegro and ascertain the proximate truth, and, if possible, penetrate to the field of hostilities.

The relations between myself and the Montenegrin authorities were such at this time, that I am morally certain that no attempt was made to mislead me on the real condition of things. The information I received, mainly from the Prince himself, was that no more than 500 Montenegrins were in Herzegovina, including the killed and wounded, nor was there in fact any need for a considerable number. The corps of Pivans was equally efficient with the best Montenegrin, and the whole Mountain furnished material quite good enough in quality for the purposes of this warfare, the great difficulty being to furnish them with arms, of which the Prince had not enough to arm all his own people. I had absolute confirmation from the chiefs Ljubibratics, Socica, Peko, and Petkovics, as well as from foreign volunteers and friends who had been in the camp at various times, that at no time previous to that of which I am speaking was there a greater number than the Prince represented, and at no subsequent time before the declaration of war did it ever pass about 700, and during the series of battles about Duga, in which Muktar figured later, there was even great exasperation against the Prince for having left the insurgents to fight alone, when he might so easily have made the struggle decisive. The actual number of combatant population which Herzegovina alone offered, and who might be classed as effective, the Prince gave me, as follows, with their chiefs, beginning at the south-east corner of the Montenegrin territory—numbers being approximate, and including all able-bodied males:—*Vasoivics* (Turkish), Panto Zemovics with 500; Mitar Vacovics, 500; Vaso Zaicics, 300; Panto Fenics, 300; *Sharanzi*, Archimandrite Dusics, 200; Josef Knezevics (Voivode), 300; band of Tripko Zacovics (killed), 300; *Yezera*, Zifko Sibalia, 300; *Duzi*, Niko Malovics, 200; *Piva*, Lazar Socica (voivode), 800; *Gatschko*, Bogdan Simonics (pope and voivode), 600; *Golia*, Gioco Visnics, 300; *Baniani*, Maxime Bacevics (voivode), 500; Chefko Peiovics, 200; Bacio Miconovics, 200; *Rudini*, Rud Alexics, 200; Bavics, 100; *Dabra*, Jovan Zombeta, 300; Gligor Milecevics, 100; Luka Miscovics, 300; Jovan Angelics, 200; *Zubci*, Bela Spaics, 400; *Cruzcoitza*, Somo Somascevics, 200. Besides these there were, from Nevesinje, Shuma, &c., about 2,000, making a total of not far from 10,000 men, of which, probably, one-half were never assembled on one occasion, and rarely more than 2,000 were involved in any actual battle, while the utmost efforts of the committees were unequal to the task of arming, munitioning, and, above all, provisioning, the numbers actually mustered. There was never a lack of men, but always of means, and I doubt if ever men in war suffered privations like theirs.

It was to be expected that the Turks would misstate the

facts, but that they would find such easy dupes amongst diplomats *was* incredible.[1]

The day after I arrived at Cettinje there came some wounded from Muratovizza. Their escort reported snow middle deep in Herzegovina, and movements difficult, and that Raouf Pasha was assembling at Gatschko forces for the revictualling of Niksics, which place, as well as Goransko, was in very great want of supplies. The latter place was by a treaty of some kind between a portion of the chiefs and Raouf supplied with a limited quantity of provisions, but Socica declared that if he must fight alone, the Turks

---

[1] SIR H. ELLIOT TO THE EARL OF DERBY.

My Lord, *Pera, January* 30, 1876.

The following account of the system pursued by the Montenegrins in aid of the Herzegovina insurgents has been communicated to me from a person in position to obtain the best information :—

All the men (in Montenegro) capable of bearing arms are considered to be soldiers, and are made into battalions of 600 men. The Commanders and Majors of these battalions, who are called Commanders and Pod-commanders, receive pay ; the remaining officers, non-commissioned officers, and men, are unpaid. When an expedition is contemplated, each man takes with him potatoes and bread, if he has any, for five days, and a reserve of provisions from each village is carried by women or baggage horses.

The Austrian committees having provided surgeons and medicines, hospitals and ambulances have been organized in some villages on the frontier.

The Prince furnishes all those who join the insurgents without authorization, but he sends about a fifth part of his effective forces into the Herzegovina. Not to overtire these poor people, His Highness takes care to change them at the end of each expedition or when their provisions are exhausted.

Reforms alone, it is stated, will never put an end to the insurrection, and force is of no avail so long as the insurgents and their Montenegrin friends have only to cross the frontier to be in safety.

I have, &c.,

(Signed) HENRY ELLIOT.

should not go to Niksics, and a council of the chiefs had refused propositions made by Raouf Pasha to permit him to pass unopposed, and decided to hold out on the Duga *coûte qui coûte.* The battle of Muratovizza was fought about the middle of November; Goransko was relieved by the treaty for two months, and the attack on Niksics was imminent. I decided to go to Niksics if possible, and watch the result.

While in Cettinje I did what I advise all who go there to do, ascend the hills to the south of the village, and study the land; for one may see nearly the whole principality at a glance, with much of Albania, the mountains of the Vasoivichi (children of Vaso) and the intervening Kutchi, and below them, spread out, like an eternal temptation to turn Turk, the ancient Montenegrin possession—the beautiful plain of the Zeta—stretching from Podgoritza all the way to the city of Scutari, though every year, owing to the thriftlessness of the Turk, some part of it is buried under the rising lake. Here Hotti, brother of Vaso, did settle, and kept his land by obedience to the Pashas and embracing Catholicism, which the Turks would tolerate.

One could see how well the border Commissions had done their work in cutting and carving for the Turk, by throwing all the districts which agriculture would claim outside the Montenegrin's boundary, and leaving him only what he could always defend. At our right was the canton of Zermnitchka; to the left, the Katunska, and Garatsch beyond, which overlooks the plain of Danilograd, and on one side protects it; in front, at our feet, the pretty valley of Dobrotskoselo, with the road winding through it to the valley of the Rieka beyond, and then a glimpse of the Rieka itself, winding through a band of meadow towards the lake.

On the edge of the plain, crowning an isolated volcanic-looking hill, was the ancient fortress of Jabliak, looking like the rather formal cup of the crater. This fort, the scene of some of the most daring feats of Montenegrin heroism, is still included in the principality by the map of Kiepert, though the Commission for defining the boundary threw it, like every other point the Turks could hold, on the Turkish side of the frontier.

It was easy to see from this point the greater part of what the Montenegrins have fought for these centuries—a poor, rocky waste of limestone, which nothing but the sheer spirit of domination should provoke any one to invade. In no other land I have ever seen is there so little earth for so much rock. In the crevices of the crumbling grey limestone stunted shrubs and trees find root, and among the fragments of the stone, slowly being split up by frost and rain, cling bouquets of wild sage and thyme, with little flowers strange to me, but which the bees know, and here and there, where a little real earth had clung or formed, clumps of a magnificent autumn crocus and scattered cyclamens. There was nothing approaching a forest and nothing resembling a plain in the whole district north of Dodosh, the frontier village under the guns of Jabliak. Down in the valley of Dobrotskoselo, at our feet, one could see how systematically the Montenegrin works for his little land: every band of earth a few feet wide being held up by a stone terrace, and the fields were really only long strips of land circling round and round to the very centre of the valley, and even there is no plain, but still terraces and terraces continually. This is one of the gardens of the principality; but there is not land enough for the amount of stone to induce an Isle of Wight gardener to pay 6*d.* an acre rent for it, if he had to do the work on it which here has been done by past generations. Down by Rieka village is, as I have said, a strip of meadow land; but, as the Turks will not drain the Scutari plain, it is being flooded with every rainy spell, and fevers depopulate the villages along it, as well as those along the lake itself, which are half the year in a swamp. This, again, is still being converted into lake, so that the boatman can see on a still day, as he floats along the surface, the villages of past generations, roads and bridges, beneath him; and along the shore are still ruins of other villages abandoned and waiting for the rising flood to bury them—after the fever the flood. And the lazy Turk, festering there in Scutari, with the water rising twice a year to his windows, has no conception that Government has duties as well as privileges, or even that his revenues would be greater by wise administration; but lets the fever eat up the people and the floods devour the land till population and desolation curse the earth for his sake. If any rational man doubts who should govern this fair scene—fair in spite of its barrenness on one side and its neglect on the other—I ask him to stand on that summit of Dobrshnja with me and see what the Montenegrin and the Turk are doing under his eyes.

Away across the plain, beyond the Zeta, rise the mountains of the Kutchi, as I have said, and there with a glass one may see Medun. From the plain rises a table land, the road up to it winding through a ravine, an ascent, perhaps, of 200 feet, and then an easy sloping pasture land, with here and there a house visible among the trees, and at the upper side, on a crag overlooking a torrent on the edge of the table land, stands Medun, looking like a crystallization of the rock it is built on. Reading of the battles which have made the locality famous even in Montenegrin annals one imagines awful ravines like the Duga, or gorges like Klek, but there was nothing here which in the distance one could consider as a formidable position—a gently sloping valley across the table land, easy heights on both sides, until it reaches Medun, where one side is sunk in the ravine over which the town looks.

CHAPTER VII.

ITH all Prince Nikita's devotion to road-making, to which he seems as much inclined as his predecessor was to military organization, it seems hardly possible that in his own day Montenegro will be a country fit for carriages, and they who would see some of the wildest and most picturesque parts of Europe must be good mountaineers, for even on horseback some of these roads are scarcely passable. The road from Cettinje to Rieka, though a tolerable zigzag and paved after a fashion, is in some parts so precipitous that the guide invites you, in your own interest, to dismount in going down, as a false step on the part of your pony would certainly send you over his head. The descent is so rapid that within an hour from Cettinje we enter the valley of Dobrotskoselo, where figs are abundant, the vine is luxuriant, the vegetation still green, and wild flowers in blossom, long after everything in the plain about Cettinje is dead and bare.

Everywhere are the same steep, rocky slopes which we found on entering the principality, and after a continuous descent for three hours we arrive at the head of the valley of Rieka proper, and see a view worth the trip. The river Rieka, after the habit of Montenegrin rivers, bursts out of the mountain already a respectable stream, and winds through a narrow plain away into the distance, where spreads the Lake of Scutari, mountain-surrounded, with the snowy peaks of the main Albanian range in the central distance. Those who visit Cettinje without the idea of penetrating further into the country should at least devote one day to Rieka, if they can get a fine one. The views are unique, and the river itself, a fountain gushing from the heart of the mountain, and its rapid course down to the winding valley beyond, with the peculiar and intense green of the waters, makes the site one to be remembered.

Rieka itself, a semi-commercial village, built along the quay, at the head of boat communication with the lake, is not especially inviting. The Prince had kindly offered me his little house to pass the night in, and as we left Cettinje after midday we entered the village only towards sunset, and, taking possession of our quarters, had a blazing fire lighted to drive out the damp. The balcony of the house overhangs the river and the curious old arched bridge, and while I sat waiting for supper and watching the sunset effect, there came a burst of merry laughter from the hill across the stream, where, with the church and its belongings, stands the school-house. School was out, and down the zigzag leading to the bridge came the liberated youngsters, sturdy, full-voiced, as rollicking a troop as ever poured out on an English village green, each one as he passed me lifting his cap with a sudden hush of awe at the foreign face and dress on the balcony. It was a finishing incident to the picture, without which justice would hardly have been done to the *ensemble*, for wherever I have been so far the school-house is almost a perpetual presence.

The morning came with a drenching rain, but a break of blue sky in the south deluded me with the hope of its clearing away, and we started about nine for Danilograd, my train consisting of a Montenegrin medical student as guide and interpreter; a servant who could speak a little Italian; one of the Prince's body-guard, delegated with enough of his authority to answer my needs, and the usual horseboys. I take the occasion to caution all travellers in this country not to make much count of Montenegrin estimates of time, for as a rule the stranger will find any journey longer by half than the time they assign to it, and so we, starting on a journey which we supposed was an easy day's ride, at nine in the morning, came in for an experience I hope never to repeat.

From Rieka the road rises rapidly, still following the river, which here is like a miniature Bosphorus, only more winding, and utterly wild. The way for hours after leaving the river is as monotonous as a hilly country can be : grey rocky ridges bristling with scrubby oaks, without a village for miles, and when at one o'clock we reached a kind of khan half-way on the journey, I decided to stop and rest, having a natural hope that the remainder of the trip would occupy no longer time. Our train was increased *en route* by a deaf-mute porter with a huge basket containing provisions and luxuries not to be hoped for from the resources of the country—tea and a samovar, white bread, and canned eat-ables, a kind afterthought of the Prince. The rain continued to pour, and after warming ourselves as best we could round the smoky fire built in the middle of the floor, as is Monte-negrin usage, we resumed our march. The road grew more rocky, with intervals of mud, but late in the afternoon, as we came up on the ridge at Koumani before beginning the descent into the valley of the Suchitza, the clouds lifted by a fortunate coincidence to show one of the loveliest valley landscapes I ever saw. The wide and fertile plain at our feet, with the mountains of Piperi beyond, and beyond them again the deep blue Berdas, whose summits still kept the clouds, was cut by two rivers, the Suchitza and the Zeta, which, united, flow into the Lake of Scutari, and which were then in flood, so that the plain was a succession of little lakes. In the south, where the plain belongs to Turkey, are the towns of Spush and Podgoritza, and here the setting sun, through an opening in the clouds, poured a great band of golden light across the plain, illuminating Podgoritza and the spurs of the mountains of the Kutchi beyond, with the flat lands to the east of the lake. To the north lay the plains of Bjelopawlitzje, the garden of Montenegro, and in the extreme distance, still cloud-capped, the mountains about Ostrog and Niksics. The view included the whole breadth of the principality from north to south.

The promise of fine weather was treacherous. The road lay down a long, rocky slope, zigzag and difficult for the horses, and the rain recommenced, so that we alternately floundered through soft mud and struggled over sharp rocks —the pedestrians far outstripping the quadrupeds, and between them came our unfortunate carrier. We had continually to wait for the horses to overtake us, and I could easily conjecture the pace of a Turkish army, and how hopeless would be a movement, when our guard could, without effort, make two miles to our actual one, while we moved without any encumbrance save our horses. We reached the plain and crossed the Suchitza by late twilight. The rain grew heavier and changed to a thunderstorm. The soil was a heavy clay, in which the animals were in great difficulty, but the pedestrians in greater, for their sandals stuck in the mud. The poor carrier, almost unable to hold

up under his load, moaned and cried like a child in the in-
articulate manner of his kind, and we had often to wait to
extricate and assist him. We had two hours' nominal
travel after crossing the river, and these two we prolonged to
more than double. The dense rain-clouds made the darkness
at times so profound that I could scarcely see my hand
before my face, and it was possible to recognize the road
only by the rare poplars at the roadside and the telegraph
poles which now and then showed against the sky. Brooks
had become torrents, and flat land one slough, in which at
length our carrier quite broke down, when, fortunately, we
discovered a light shining through the crevices of a roadside
cottage, where we deposited him with his load, and, mounting our guardsman on the horse of the domestic, we committed the *impedimenta* of all kinds to the scanty shelter of
the hovel and pushed on, we three, for Danilograd. By
this we were drenched, weary, and, but for the quicker
sense of our horses, lost. Night had become utter darkness,
and the rain, unmitigated, deluged everything, the road
itself becoming, if possible, still more obscure by passing
through tracts of forest, and there was nothing for it but to
trust to our guard's general knowledge of the country and
the horses' instinct of the way, give them the bridle, and
commit ourselves to Providence. It was only when flashes
of lightning lighted up the path that we knew we were on it,
and I have no knowledge of how the time passed, for it
seemed hours while we were making the last two or three
miles of the way. Our horses carried us into Danilograd,
however, before all the village had extinguished its lights,
and the only functionary we could arouse committed us to
the hospitality of a more prosperous neighbour, who gave us
a cordial welcome, a supper of trout from the Zeta, and a

bed on the floor, where I passed a night even more miserable than the day.

Danilograd is a new village, reminding one of the new towns in Western America, with a large ground plan and a very slight filling-up, and will, no doubt, one of these days, be the central and most important city of Montenegro. A fine carriage-road is in construction from Cattaro, branching from the Cettinje road at Njegush, and a good bridge crosses the Zeta, the road passing over which branches south to Spush and north to Ostrog. The valley is fertile, and seems to favour the vine and maize, while figs are abundant, and fields of a most luxuriant tobacco were still fresh and in bloom. The village is the seat of an agricultural school, the first of its kind in Slavonia. The whole valley of the Zeta is charming, and affords fine trout fishing, like all the streams which empty into the lake of Scutari. The fish here run as high as 40 lbs., while in the lake they have been caught as heavy as 60 lbs. The way to Ostrog follows the river nearly to its source, which, like the Rieka, is an immense fountain. There are no brooks by the roadside, but huge water-sources here and there gushing out of the apparently solid rock, the issue of the katavothra, through which the waters of the table lands above disappear. The valley narrows until it ends in a vast, irregular semicircle of mountains, high up on one of which, like a mud swallow's-nest, in a cavity of the perpendicular cliff, is the Sanctuary of Ostrog, the upper convent, it is generally called ; but it is now only a hermitage and sacred place, tenanted by an old priest, whose duty it is to watch the body of St. Basil, which lies here in a sarcophagus of carved wood, and to administer the rites to the crowds of the faithful who climb up here on the great *fêtes*, especially that of the Virgin. The actual convent is about two-thirds of the way up to the shrine, and is a most comfortable and hospitable retreat. It cost us an hour and a half's hard climbing to get to it by the muddy road, and the sun had already set when we entered the gates.

Monks are famous for the admirable selection of their convent sites, and Ostrog is one of the best chosen I have visited. It looks down on the valley from an elevation of about 2,000 feet, and is open only to the west wind. The land about it is the richest mountain land I have seen in Montenegro, the rock being a very rotten slate, and broken into a succession of plateaux, which form so many little pasture lands or arable fields. Above the convent all is forest of oak or chestnut until we reach the foot of the limestone cliff in which is the sanctuary. For picturesque variety of rock and tree, mountain and valley, for the abundance of material such as a painter would delight in—rock of massive, grandiose form, and trees quaint and weather-tormented, the hill-side about Ostrog surpasses anything I know. The lower convent is now of more importance in a political point of view than a religious, for there are only two monks, both of whom are of an order more militant than devotional, and Ostrog is the frontier fortress, and the terminus of the telegraph, by which comes all the intelligence from the region beyond the Tara, the district between Plevlié and Novi-Bazaar. It is four hours from here to Niksics.

Upper Ostrog was the scene of one of the most heroic defences of Montenegrin history. Here, in 1853, Mirko, father of the present Prince, with thirty-two of his voivodes and chiefs, was driven and besieged for nineteen days by a large Turkish army. The hermitage was then a fortress as well, when need was, and contained supplies of arms,

provisions, and ammunition, in addition to which Mirko
employed all his men during the time that the Turkish army
was closing in on them, in carrying huge stones up to the
gallery. The only way to get at the Montenegrins was by
direct assault on a narrow staircase cut in the solid rock.
Those who attempted the entrance were either crushed in
the mass by the stones thrown from above, or shot through
the loopholes or from the head of the staircase. One of
the defenders was killed early in the siege, and finding it
necessary to dispose of the body, they let it out of the win-
dow by cords, and to prevent the Turks from mutilating it,
they let down one of the chiefs to bury it. The assailants
discovering him before he could be drawn back, he ran for
it, made his way through the besieging army, and carried the
news to Danilo, who raised an army and relieved his general
and his comrades. Two of the little garrison were killed,
and 750 Turks, partly in a battle between two detachments,
each of which in the darkness mistook the other for a body
of Montenegrins. This was regarded as the effect of the
intervention of St. Basil, and of course the whole defence
was largely attributed to the favour of the saint. This
shrine enjoys an extensive reputation as a miraculous agent.
At the great *festa* of the Virgin, thousands came here from
all parts of the Balkan. The cures reported are of Turks as
well as believers, and the reverence of the saint by the Mussulmans of Herzegovina and Albania is almost, if not quite,
as profound as that of the Christians. We were allowed to
see the body in its wrappings, and one hand was uncovered
as a special favour.

I hoped to have penetrated to Niksics from here, but the
Superior told me that it was to the last degree unsafe, as the
plain about the town was infested by bands of Mussulmans

in great want of everything a stranger would be likely to
have with him, and who pay no respect to any authority,
or any distinction, except that of greater military strength.
I was obliged to renounce entirely any movement beyond
here, not only for the reason above given, but from a heavy
snowfall, which made the mountain roads utterly impracticable.

The day of our ride to Ostrog was the one fair-day oasis
of our journey. All the time we remained there the rain
fell in the valley, and the snow on the high mountains,
until, in sheer despair, we started to return, still in drenching rain, which accompanied us to Danilograd, whence I
intended to make the detour round by the lake to Scutari. The
sirdar in command at Danilograd assured me, as the Prince
had before leaving Cettinje, that it would not be possible for
Montenegrins to accompany me through Albania, as the
journey would probably be ended for them by decapitation,
and really I found that no Montenegrin would consent to
accompany me only as far as Podgoritza, as even if my
presence protected him while going, he had slender chance of
returning, alone. Nor would they even let me horses to go
with. My interpreter, a venturesome young fellow, decided
to go on, and run the risk; and, if possible, see Scutari
before dying. To shorten the journey I telegraphed to
Cettinje to ask the Prince to send me his little steam-launch
to the lake shore, then found a Rayah of Podgoritza, who
had come to market at Danilograd, and rigging substitutes for
saddles, with the Rayah himself as guide, and, changing
Gosdanovics' Montenegrin cap for a felt hat, and putting him
under charge to diminish his knowledge of Serb to the
minimum of our needs, to notice nothing, and only reply
when there was absolute necessity, I set out for Spush

(pronounced Spuss), the frontier Turkish town on the south. The road changed from mud and overflowed meadows to an ancient causeway, so worn and dilapidated that the horses preferred the worst side-path to keeping on the stones. There had been no repairs made on it since it was made, I conjecture, and there were actually portions where the ridge of pavement rose, like a lean hog's back, to an isolated elevation of several feet above the more trodden paths on each side.

At the entrance of the town we were stopped by the guard, curious to know what was our business, where we came from, &c. There was no gate, only a guard-house by the wayside, an exaggerated sentry-box, under cover of which the sentinel stood and made merry over our ridiculous plight, as we sat on our muddy horses, ourselves splashed and dripping, the rain pouring down all the time in torrents. We must wait there until the slow-going messenger could walk to the other end of the town, where the chief of the Zapties held his court, and ask what was to be done with us. One of the guard did me the honour to ask about passports, and looked at mine much as a magpie might look at a piece of bright metal, turned it over and returned it to me with an uncomprehending " Peki," and then we waited in silence. Presently, the messenger returned, saying that we were to go to the Zaptieh. Here we found the usual Turk—a Binbashi, but as grave and polite as a Pasha ; the same courteous and impassible person a Turk always is when he is not "put out"—sympathetic and interesting. Quite the contrary were two secretaries, Mussulmans of the country, whose frank and unabated malignity did not wait for words, but glared out at their eyes in a manner not at all unfamiliar. I took my seat on the divan, made my salaam, and replied

by dumb show to the questions of which I could gather
the import from the circumstances, and keeping the interdict
on the tongue of my companion, gave the Binbashi to understand that I was from England and going to Podgoritza, and
thence to Scutari. We tried English, French, and Italian
in vain, and then he bethought himself of sending for the
Doctor, an Italian, when a bright-looking Lieutenant standing by bethought himself of Romaic, which was an immense
relief, though he understood very little of it, as it enabled
me to say that I was from London, the correspondent of an
English journal, and that my companion was my *gram-
maticos;* that I had come from Ragusa, as the Turkish
visa on my passport obtained there showed, only it was in
French, and none of them could read anything of it but the
seal, if they could that; but the Romaic did not allow of
our going into the philosophy of travel far enough to make
any of them understand why I had come to that out-of-the
way place at such a time and in such weather, and, above
all, from Montenegro. However, it enabled me to expatiate
on the old friendship of England for the Porte, and mollified
matters considerably. Then the Doctor came, and we were
enabled to appease the suspicions of my trustworthiness by
explaining the nature of newspaper correspondence and the
interest England took in the state of the country, and
gratified everybody with my opinion that diplomacy would
soon interfere and stop the fighting; for here, as elsewhere,
I found the Mussulmans weary of the war, whether the
ordinary population or the military classes.

Meanwhile, and while the Romaic was going on, my
Montenegrin was mute, and understood nothing of the prin-
cipal performance, but heard the by-play of the Serb
Mussulmans. "Bah," said one of the secretaries to the

other, "I could, with a stick, kill twenty such men as these, and would do it too, if I dared; such rubbish as they are! I would like to send them all to the devil." The other replied that he would like nothing better than just such fun; and then he added that I was certainly a stranger, but he was sure that he had seen my companion somewhere, and he had very grave suspicions of him that he was a Montenegrin, especially as I had explained that I came *viâ* Cettinje. "No," said the other, "that is not likely; no Montenegrin dares come here now." The real cause of my arrest and the annoyance I was put to was simply my having come from Montenegro. Yet in June, 1876, the Grand Vizier denied that any hindrance had existed.[1]

When the Doctor came we launched into general politics, drank another cup of coffee each, smoked another cigarette, and begged to be allowed to retire with the *visa* of the Bin-bashi, which being graciously accorded, we remounted our steeds and filed through the streets to the bridge, and so across and on our way to Podgoritza along the Zeta. The river here runs through a deep channel cut through massive conglomerate and a little lower down unites with the Moratscha, famous for its trout, the best of the country.

Podgoritza, a straggling dilapidated town, much given to ruin, is approached by curious circuitous ways, with excellent defences as against old methods of assault, but with walls

---

[1] "I will finally say, my Prince, that our authorities have never had the intention of preventing the communications of the principality with the outside world. The proof of this is that they continue uninterrupted, and that the Montenegrins go freely, and without being in any way molested, to Spouze, to Podgoritza, and to Scutari. From what precedes your Highness will see that the Sublime Porte has not adopted any measure which can pre-occupy or disquiet Montenegro."—*Grand Vizier to Nikita, June* 25, 1876, Blue Book.

crumbling and dilapidated. I had to show my passport
again in crossing the bridge over the Moratscha, and on
entering the town naturally went to the best and only clean
khan, one kept by an Orthodox Christian. We had to sleep
in Podgoritza, and start early next morning for Plamnitza,
on the shore of the lake, where the Prince of Montenegro
had, in compliance with my request, ordered the little
steamer from Rieka to meet us and convey us to Scutari.
We were wet, cold, and fasting, and it was the middle of
the afternoon ; but we waited in vain for either fire or food
for half an hour, when our Podgoritzan guide returned and
informed us that we could not stay at that khan, that there
was no room (it seemed to me quite empty, and we had
been told on arriving that we could stay), but that the Miralai
had appointed a place for us. G., who travelled under a
Russian passport, passed as a Muscovite, and was stated to
be such by the Podgoritzan, and this allowed a little knowledge of Serb, which now became indispensable. We passed
through the greater part of the town to a small, decayed, and
dirty khan, the head-quarters of the chief of police, who, with
many compliments, assured us that he was so anxious that
we should be comfortable, that he had assigned us quarters
next his own (in the police office), and, inviting us to sit
down round his mangal and dry ourselves over his charcoal
fire, gave orders to clean out the room adjoining—a kind
of closet, about 14ft. by 10ft., on the floor of which the
dust of months lay undisturbed. While the attendant
obeyed his orders, we were put through another inquisition
in his room, while he gave orders in Serb for our dinner and
treatment to the keeper of the khan in such a way that,
while he seemed to be paying compliments he was really
consigning us to imprisonment. He had two or three

persons in his suite who spoke Italian, and so I was able to explain fully all that I cared to explain of my business and intentions. He took my passport and sent it to the Commandant de Place, who returned it as all right; but they were not at all sure about my intentions in going to Scutari. G., who now and then spoke a few words of very bad Serb, was able to hear again all the by-talk and the orders given to telegraph to Scutari as to the disposal of us, and for putting a guard at the door of the khan to prevent any one coming to see us. My boots had given out, and I asked to have some sent in to try. The order was given by them with great ostentation, but when they came there was only one pair, and those not large enough for a boy of fourteen; there were no others, I was assured. I took it all in good part, and humoured the fraud as if I saw nothing.

We had to answer for every step of our journey, and the connection of our movements with Cettinje was what none of them could understand. They did not believe that the Montenegrin steamer was coming for us, and it was finally settled that we were to go to Plamnitza, with a guide, as we were informed, but, as we learnt from the by-talk, under the custody of a guard, which was to keep us in sight, proceed to extremes if we attempted to escape from them, and if the steamer was not there, to bring us back to the same quarters immediately. I was courteously invited, therefore, to return to Podgoritza in case I did not find the steamer there, as it would be unsafe to cross the lake in a boat, and was assured that I might count confidently on the attention and protection of the Zaptieh.

We were then shown our room, on the floor of which was spread a fragment of old carpet, with a dirty blanket for mattress and another for covering, a mangal filled with lighted charcoal was brought in, and the supper followed—a boiled fowl, with the water in which it was boiled thickened with vermicelli, wine, and brown bread—and we were left alone. The servant came in again and cleared away our supper when we had finished. The prison routine was finished all but locking up, yet we had not been ten minutes by ourselves, when one of the Christians of the town (a Catholic, moreover) came in, and in a stealthy visit managed to tell me in Italian how miserable the Christian population was, how blind (*cieco* was his word), and how hopeless. We went to our blankets, having nothing else to do, and before I had a chance to sleep I heard the bolts of our outside door shot, and realized that we were really imprisoned for the night; but as the horses had been ordered for the early dawn, I gave myself no anxiety. Naturally I slept little, however, and all night it seemed to me that Podgoritza was peopled by cocks, who continually insisted on making believe that it was daybreak. We got off next morning without further molestation, and had a weary ride of four hours through the rain, which still poured pitilessly; and my anxiety lest the steamer should not have come, or having come should have gone again, and we so be compelled to make all those weary miles of mud and rain again, back to Danilograd and Rieka, or wait a few days under guard in Podgoritza, can easily be imagined, and that it was not decreased by G. understanding the dialogue of our two Mussulman-Serb Zapties, which ran on the degradation of having to make such a journey, in pelting rain, for a couple of Ghiaours, whose heads they would have been much better pleased at cutting off than protecting. The cutting off our heads was, in fact, the burden of their conversation.

We found the engineer of the steamer waiting for us in

the village, and, after an hour's canoeing out towards the open water, discovered the steamer tied to a branch of a tree whose tops alone showed above the water. Instead, however, of taking us to Scutari, she was obliged to go back for fuel to Rieka, where we passed the night, and started afresh, this time in company with the French Consul at Scutari, to whose presence I was indebted for being able to land that night, as we were overhauled by a boat from the man-of war off the city, which, finding the Consul on board, landed us all without further question, though the rule of the port forbade our steamer going up to the landing after the sunset hour. The landing, indeed, was far up in the streets, for all the lower part of the town was under water, and it was late in the evening when we found a room in the dirtiest khan I have ever been in, but the proprietor of which, an Albanian, made amends for the meagreness of our supper and the very indifferent character of his beds by cordiality and an effort to do his best.

So much for the itinerary of a journey which it would be difficult to induce me to repeat under the same difficulties and conditions, and of the latter part of which I only retain a general impression, the state of the weather, and the suspiciousness of the authorities, preventing me from learning much of the country or anything of the disposition of the people. The former is to a large extent under water, and the latter, so far as I could judge from demeanour and externals, would be better under ground. Montenegro showed much poverty, but the transition to Turkish territory produced a painful impression of squalor and wretchedness—listlessness in the people, obsequiousness, and want of that self-confidence so marked in the Montenegrin. The thought constantly recurred to me that the love of life must be very

strong in these people to make them content to live such an
existence. I saw fields of magnificent tobacco standing
with the leaves rotting and stems crushed down, cattle
grazing through them, the fertile lands all round the lake
of Scutari from one to ten feet under water, roads all in an
extreme state of dilapidation, and even the fortresses crumbling. Everything was toned by decay.

I called the second day after arriving on the Governor of
Scutari, Eshref Pasha, a most amiable and interesting man,
and, *rara avis* among Turkish Pashas, a man of letters and
a poet, the second in rank in Turkey, I was told. He
laughingly asked me, after salutations, if I had been at
Podgoritza, which gave me the opportunity to say that I
had not come to complain of that affair, but to pay my
respects to a fellow *littérateur*. His broad, good-humoured
face and keen black eyes lighted up with a natural pleasure,
and he asked how I had learnt that he was of the craft,
which paved the way for more pleasant words ; and, for an
exception in my official visits, we did not talk politics or
military matters. Secretaries and messengers were continually running in and out with papers to sign and orders
to be made out. Conversation on poetry filled up the inter-
spaces, and I remarked that he must have very little time
for literary pursuits with all the official pressure on his time
and energies. "Yes," he said, "poetry is my refuge in the
night, when I am unable to sleep—I have no other time."
I hoped that I might have the pleasure some day of seeing
some example of his muse in an English dress, but he said,
what we all know, that translation is mostly destructive to
poetry. I begged him to favour me with a copy of a poem,
and said I would do my best to get it properly translated,
adding that London was rich in men of condition equal even to

H

translating poetry, and that if something of the poem must be inevitably lost, at least the substance of the thought would remain. He finally read me very pleasantly a short poem in Turkish, of which I understood not a word, but the movement of which was certainly full of dignity and possessed a marked and characteristic melody, and promised to send a copy to my address next morning, but his official character was fatal to any promise, and the poem was like Turkish reforms, it never came.

The Pasha is evidently one of those misplaced links in an unequal chain whose strength is no greater than its weakest part. As we did not talk of politics, and I had no desire to know the Turkish version of all the news, I was not able to judge of his political capacity. He seemed a well-meaning man, sympathetic, and capable, under a good system, of doing routine work in Government machinery. There may be many such under the surface of Turkish disorganization, buried out of sight and hope in the mass of fanaticism and ignorant pride.

Scutari was in an extensively flooded condition, and the question of the day was not of the barometer or exchange, but of the increase of the water in the market-place. "It rose four fingers' breadth yesterday," I heard one merchant remark to another. I saw a man fishing in a roadside ditch, who had a fine basket of carp to show as his take. And all because the Drin has filled up its old way to the sea, from the bar never having been dredged out, and sets back into the Lake of Scutari and through the Boyana to the sea.

It may be worth while to add, before leaving Eshref Pasha, that when, some months later, the new Iradé was issued and ordered to be published in the provinces, he took it in good faith, and immediately put it into practice by calling on the people to make their elections and state the needs of their community. They replied at once by indicating the reopening of the Drin, so as to drain the Lake of Scutari, making of better roads, and construction of a railway from Scutari to Antivari. Perhaps the contemplation of these actual consequences of the rash belief of a Governor in the seriousness of the Iradé led to Eshref's removal. The Porte is not accustomed to being taken at its word, and there is no knowing what might happen if the poet had many imitators in his serious way of looking at things.

Eshref was replaced by Hamdi, our old Bosniak functionary, dismissed for doing nothing in Herzegovina.

CHAPTER VIII.

RAOUF PASHA occupied the whole of the latter half of November and nearly all December getting his expedition to Niksics organized, and then attacked the Duga with forces reported at 12,000 to 16,000 men. The army was divided into two divisions, of which one was to fight its way through, and when in possession of the passes, the other, escorting the provisions, was to follow. Raouf, commanding the former, made his attack, and was met by Socica, who stopped him at Krstaz. Raouf took strong defensive positions and waited two days, when Socica's men, receiving neither aid nor provisions from Peko, who commanded the main body of the insurgents, and on some frivolous pretext held aloof from the fighting, were obliged to evacuate the position they held, and Raouf went through without further opposition. Peko took his revenge by an attack on the cattle of the Turkish army at Plana, in the rear of the two armies, and carried off an immense booty ; but his defection from Socica at the critical moment produced an alienation between the two chiefs which lasted for months, and was only healed finally by Socica's being assured that Peko had only obeyed secret orders in not attacking the Turks, it being considered in certain official quarters that it was inexpedient to bring matters to an issue between the Porte and Montenegro; but Socica was not docile in these matters, and would not have accepted such orders even directly from the Prince of Montenegro, while these came from Russian authorities, for whom Peko had unlimited reverence, and Socica at that time very little.

This was the first indication I had been able to get of any direct intervention of Russian officials in the affair. This, moreover, was certainly not hostile to the Turks, and could scarcely be considered anything more than pacific intervention, but it marked a change in the direction of affairs. It coincided, moreover, with the sending of the important Russian and Swiss Red Cross expeditions to Cettinje, and the increased recognition of the insurrection by the public opinion of Russia. Large subscriptions were being made for the insurrection, and the agents of the Slavonic committees appeared in greater activity than we had dreamed of before. I am of opinion that it was at this time that the Russian influence became dominant over the others, and from that day this influence increased. It was not, however, an official direction, which was not apparent until about the date of the presentation of the Andrassy note. At the time of which I am now writing, the agents of the committees were far from being agreed with the official agents, and I became on several occasions witness of the hostility between the two, and of the former I must say that they were for the most part full of an enthusiasm which did its work with the insurgents. The public opinion in Russia was, however, beginning to produce its effect on the officials, the farthest from the throne being soonest swept away by it; but the movement once begun, it was impossible that the officials should not be influenced in their conduct by it, and, as we see, it finally involved the throne itself. Jonine, who was the immediate agent in any properly diplomatic dealings, was less in favour at the camp of the insurgents than the agents who were with them, fought with them, and shared their rations with them, and between Jonine and certain of these there was implacable feud. They are probably, more than any other cause, responsible for the obstinacy of the insurgents in the interval just previous to the Andrassy propositions being made. Men don't require much encouragement to go the way of their inclinations, and it was inevitable that the official agents should in time overbid the unofficial, or lose control.

Early in January, 1876, winter suddenly set in with great rigour at Ragusa, and on the sea-coast the weather was the coldest remembered by any living person. The sufferings of the insurgents were grave, but those of the Turkish troops frightful. In the high country about Gatschko snow impeded all movements, and many soldiers were found frozen to death. I saw at Ragusa deserters from the army of Shefket Pasha, who described their condition as so bad that the bulk of the army would have deserted if they knew that they could get to Austria and not be remanded to their standards. Operations were entirely paralyzed.

Towards the end of January the winter began to moderate, and the bands prepared to take the field again, while Raouf Pashà was recalled and replaced by Achmet Muktar, for the reason, it was said, that Raouf not only told the Porte that its army was not in condition to attack Montenegro, but even that the insurgents were to a great extent justified by the misgovernment which they had suffered under, in rising in revolt. He was sent to Crete in more or less disgrace.

Muktar came, breathing fire and the sword, menacing the population with all the horrors Bulgaria has since experienced. He made a military promenade through Herzegovina, saw nothing, and went back for the remainder of the winter to Mostar. The time had come, however, when the Montenegrin Government, acting under the menace of the Turks to take the principality in hand when they finished the insurrection, and encouraged (or excited) by the Russian committees and volunteers, and probably by officials as well, felt emboldened to allow a more efficient aid to the movement, and the remnant of the original Montenegrin corps, reduced by death and wounds to about 150, was recalled and replaced by several hundred new men; and the Prince, by his attitude towards the insurgents, showed that he was disposed to yield to the popular feeling, by taking more or less the control of the affair into his hands—at least, advising it in its policy and diplomacy; and Vukotics, the oldest Montenegrin captain, took the direction of its affairs. The bands were advised to leave the Montenegrin frontier, and descended, to the number of about 1,500 men, to the Trebinje plain, under the command of Peko. He established himself at the old camp of Grebci, driving out Ljubibratics and his *entourage;* and on the Greek New Year's Day (12th January), I met him with two or three others of the chiefs at the midnight supper at the house of Monteverde, in Ragusa, his only visit to the city during the whole insurrection, and the only one of either of the proper chiefs of the Mountain, except Milecevics, whom I met several times. Socica remained at Piva.

Peko disposed his force on the road between Trebinje and Ragusa, and a provision expedition coming from the latter place was, on January 17th, compelled to turn back to prevent capture. The next day, the Turks—five battalions, with 400 *indigènes* and six guns, as I learned from the Austrian military authorities—marched out from Trebinje, and leaving their guns, for greater security, with a detachment on the Trebinje side of Duzi, the rest came as far as the positions indicated to be occupied for the protection of the provision train to come through next day; and having posted two companies, believed to be a total of 180 men, and constructed breastworks for them, set out on their return to the city. It had been the intention of Peko to allow the troops perfect liberty of movement until the provision train came out from Ragusa; but seeing this fortification of the positions taken, he concluded at once that the thing must be stopped, and marched with the men at hand to the position from which the battle is named—Radovan-Zdrielo—an inconsiderable hill about midway between the fortress of Drien, near the Austrian frontier, and that of Duzi; somewhat less than half the distance between Ragusa and Trebinje from the latter place. Here he gave the signal for the attack, which began with about 250 men, increasing, as the other bands came up, to about 800. But at the first shots fired, the troops began a precipitate retreat, and, firing a few shots behind them, fled in utter disorder back towards Trebinje, the insurgents pursuing and cutting them down. The pursuit continued until the fortress of Duzi was reached, when the flying column communicated the panic to the reserve, and the fight continued to the city, the pursuit stopping at Duzi. The number of Turkish dead left on the road, according to the tale of the noses brought to Peko, was 250.

Peko now turned his attention to the force posted to hold the road, and, finding the defences too strong for direct assault, he placed a strong cordon around it, and waited until the next day. Tripko Vukalovics was sent down the road with his men, to watch any movement from Trebinje,

and another party towards Drien. With the exception of a
slight fusillade nothing was done the next day.

When the news came in to Ragusa, Colonel Monteverde
(correspondent of the "Russki Mir," and agent for the Slavonic committees of St. Petersburg), and myself decided at
once to go out to the battlefield, and, if possible, witness the
expected sortie from Trebinje; but delay in starting and
then in finding horses at Ombla kept us until it was too late
to reach the camp before dark, and we therefore prepared
for an early start next morning. We left at early light; and
after a seven hours' walk over the hardest ground I have
ever seen, even in that hard country, we began to hear, far
off, the muttering of musketry. On reaching Vukovics, the
general head-quarters, we found an ambulance, which owed
its existence to the "Russki Mir" and its correspondent,
and the preliminary attention being given to some wounded
by a young Russian medical student, who, when his dress-
ings were done, took his rifle and accompanied us to Peko's
temporary quarters near the beleaguered positions. The
scouts who joined us on the way reported that a column had
just debouched by the Popovo-polje, coming from Stolatz to
Trebinje, which would arrive at the latter place about
2 p.m., making it certain that no movement in relief would
be made that day. We arrived about half-past two at the
abandoned village—hamlet rather, for there are not above
ten houses in it—which was the quarters of Peko and as
many of the insurgents as could sleep there. Here we
halted a few minutes to depose all superfluous loading and
make inquiries. The fusillade echoed through the mountains with an unintermitting roar, and the cries of the chiefs
of the insurgents exciting their men could be heard above
the sound of the musketry.

I think I was never so utterly fatigued in my life; but the hope of seeing the position of affairs, and getting horses in time to get back that night, drove us on, without stopping to rest, over the mountain which shelters the village from the Trebinje road, from the further slopes of which we could see what was going on. As we climbed the slope, a nearly spent rifle-ball sang over our heads and down into the valley beyond the village, indicating tolerably our distance, and that we were in the line of somebody's fire. We hurried on beyond the ridge, and came in sight of the beleaguered hill. It was the first of a series of conical undulations which culminate, in the direction of Ragusa, at Drien, not above 100 feet high, with two peaks, between which ran the Trebinje road. The wind, which was very light, blew from us, and we could see every flash of the rifles on our side of the slope and on the ridge. The mass of the insurgents were on the side furthest from us, and theirs were the balls which, passing over the hill, reached as far as where we were. The summit was encircled with a line of smoke; and when we first came in view, the downward flashes extended down the side seen in profile, the upward jets of smoke not being so plainly distinguished. It was clear that there were no insurgents to speak of on our side of the hill itself, but that on the further side and on the slopes seen in profile the upward fire was climbing. The fire of the garrison was incessant; but as both parties were fighting from cover, we could not distinguish individuals, nor amid the grey rocks which cover the hill distinguish the men from the rocks. We could see the tents on the summit, however; and while we were watching, suddenly the flashes of upward smoke appeared halfway up the slope, and the fire seemed to break out into new vigour, and the cries and the fusillade mingled again with intensified rage. The line of assault had moved up to the lower breastwork, and there was a hand-to-hand fight across it, and then the fire of the assailants and defenders could be distinguished again, the former converging from a distance, apparently not above fifty yards, on the diminished circle of defence, the insurgents having reversed the breastwork, and used it in attacking the upper work. Here was killed one of the bravest of the brave, Maxime Bacevics, voivode of Baniani, shot through the breast; and here were men wounded on the insurgent side, for the first time, so far as I can learn, by bayonet or sword. Some of the assailants were wounded fearfully by stones thrown down on them, and the wounded began to come in past where we were sitting. One man came along walking slowly, but alone, with both hands cut across at the back, a gash in the neck, and a ball through the thigh, just clearing the hip joint. He showed us with a grim satisfaction the nose of the Turk who had given him the cuts, as did several others of the wounded.

The afternoon was magnificent—nothing could be finer than the weather, in fact—sky cloudless, just a breath of northerly wind, and the crocuses and snowdrops in bloom on the sunny side of every elevation, while the snow lay undisturbed in the shade. In the distance were the snow-covered peaks of the Crnagora, and all around us the grey hills of Herzegovina, scantily flecked with the brown-leaved trees and shrubs which find occasional existence, or low, broad juniper bushes. Beneath us was the plain through which the Trebinje road runs, and at our right the slope on which the road rises to the ridge where the fort of Drien stands, on the platform of which we could distinguish with the naked eye the garrison moving uneasily about. At the left the road wound through the rolling ground, and was lost to sight; but beyond, we could distinguish the blockhouses at Duzi, and at the end of the plain, where it seemed to be hemmed in by the hills, was Trebinje, its grey houses shining in the sun, and the river gleaming in sudden turns here and there. Still further to the left was the Popovo-polje, and here and there we could catch the cries of the shepherds and goatherds to their flocks. Whether from the strange and violent contrast between the sunny, tranquil nature and the shouting of the excited combatants below me, the knowledge of the slaughter going on at the moment, the occasional reminder in the moaning balls that wandered our way that the whole affair was dread earnest, the sight of the wounded men coming in—perhaps even in part from the natural sympathy with the hapless garrison, around whom a pitiless death was closing slowly, and who still held out with heroic obstinacy, or whether from the nervousness of the position, exaggerated by excessive fatigue—the whole thing excited in me a disgust and horror I never before in my life experienced, though it was neither my first experience under fire nor of this kind of fighting. The most vividly conscious feeling in all this *mélange* was pity for the brave men on the hill.

The afternoon was closing in, and there was no sign of movement from Trebinje. The wounded were coming in faster, and the path was marked with blood drops, and those who came in with the wounded confirmed the opinion that no assault would be given that day, although the fire was still unslackened. Almost every wounded man had an amputated nose to show, and they all said that there were many killed and wounded, and more of the former than the latter. Most of the wounded we saw were hit by balls in the head and neck. Perovics—a Herzegovinian priest, who distinguished himself for gallantry at Muratovizza—here received a wound in the head, and his brother one in the neck. I felt ashamed to do nothing for the wounded, but I was scarcely able to drag myself along, and I doubt not they were, in spite of their wounds, as able-bodied as I for the moment, and in fact they took the matter in extreme nonchalance, only one or two whom I saw showing any symptom of suffering; but we went back to the village with a number of them, who told us the details of the fight.

Peko still remained on the battlefield. There were no horses but his, and these no one dared send for without his permission, and, beside, they were at Vukovics; so we slowly settled down to the conclusion that the only thing to be done was to pass the night in camp. The firing ceased at sunset, and the body of Maxime was brought in before dark, amid general and evidently heartfelt lamentation. His own men wept like children, and it was very easy to see there was an extraordinary devotion felt towards the man by his followers and his fellow-captains. "A thousand Turks dead would not pay us for Maxime"—was the wail of old Peko, and his men swore a bloody vengeance for the morrow.

All the long evening the men were coming in from the battlefield clamorously discussing the feats of this man and that other, the heroism of one or the other chief; the reliefs arming and going out, and, our cabin being the head-quarters, all the chiefs came in one by one through the evening, and Peko and Luka about eleven, when we got the report of the day's doings. The Turks had occupied and fortified both peaks, and made a double line of stone wall around the higher one. The lower peak being closely approached, and the force on it, seeing capture inevitable, evacuated the summit and ran for the higher, about sixty being caught and killed *en route* by the insurgents. The lower barricade was then attacked in the same way and finally carried, and all the dispositions made for an assault early next morning. Peko judged that there were about fifty of the garrison still alive, but these could with their breech-loaders do a great deal of damage before they were overpowered. However, it was necessary to finish with these before the troops came out from Trebinje, so he should order an attack *à l'arme blanche* early next morning. After eating their supper of beef, roasted on sticks before the fire, and drinking raki, they went on discussing the deeds of the day, until, stunned by the clamour of voices, which all seemed going at once, and each trying to drown the others, I wrapped myself in my shawl and lay down on the stone platform which surrounded the fireplace, and served, without even straw, as bed, and went soundly to sleep, in spite of smoke almost stifling, shouting, snoring, and all physical discomfort.

When I woke it was daylight, and Peko came in to say that the scouts had come in reporting that the remnant of the garrison had escaped during the night; as he then supposed, going to Trebinje, but, as we afterwards found, partly going to Drin, and being nearly all cut down by the insurgent guard on the road, others wandering off into the hills, and three or four came into Ragusa.

In the two days' fighting, *i.e.*, that on the road and the attack of the fortified position, the total Turkish loss was about 400 killed and 300 wounded who arrived at Trebinje, every one who did not being put to the sword, after the manner of those battles on both sides. The insurgent loss was about 100 killed and badly wounded, the latter being all brought to Ragusa.

The loss of Maxime Bacevics was a very grave one, though
he had never taken a leading part in military affairs owing
to his youth, as he was related to the Prince of Montenegro
(an immense element of moral authority with his people),
and was a hero of that type which always most strongly
dominates such a warlike race—brave to rashness, politic,
with exceptional physical powers, and the son of a brave
man killed, as Maxime was, fighting with the Turks. His
body was brought to Ragusa, where the demonstration and
honours given to it at the funeral became the subject of
diplomatic remonstrance.[1] The streets were hung with

[1] Sir H. Elliot to the Earl of Derby.

My Lord, *Constantinople, February* 14, 1876.

The account of the encouragement and countenance given to the insurgents at Ragusa greatly exceeds all that I was prepared for.

The Russian Consulate is the open resort of the insurgent chiefs ;
their correspondence is sent to the Consul, who is a party to all their
projects, and associates himself intimately with them.

He does not appear to make an attempt to conceal the part he is
playing, for on the occasion of the death of the Chief Maxime, in one
of the late encounters, the Russian flag at the Consulate was hoisted at
half-mast, and M. Jonine himself joined the funeral procession (!)

With such acts as these it is not surprising that the insurgents should
suppose their attempt to be fully approved by the Russian Government,
for they can hardly be expected to believe that an accredited agent would
venture upon them without knowing that it meets with the approval of
his superior authorities.

Some of the wounded when asked why they continue to struggle, when
the Porte is ready to grant all their demands, have answered plainly that
they are bound to go on as long as they are told by Russia to do so (!!)

The assurances given at St. Petersburg of the wish of the Imperial
Government that the insurgents would lay down their arms, must
naturally go for nothing as long as its official representative, with
whom they are in communication, encourages them to go on.

I have, &c.,

(Signed) Henry Elliot.

The above is a fair example of the curious misrepresentation which
perplexed public opinion. None of the insurgent chiefs were allowed to

the Slav tricolour, and the popular demonstration was as imposing as that which had welcomed the Emperor to Dalmatia.

visit the Russian Consulate at any time—if they met Jonine it was at Monteverde's, and this very rarely, so far as I know or believe only once —the Greek New Year. Jonine did not join in the funeral procession, for I myself accompanied it, and saw him on his balcony as it passed. The funeral was on Sunday, and all the consuls, except the Turkish, had their flags hoisted, as is the custom in honour of the day; but as the day was one of absolute calm, the flags hung to the masts like ropes, and Jonine distinctly denied half-masting his flag. A similar complaint was made of the English Consul, and he received a despatch from Sir Henry Elliot asking an explanation, though I am able to declare, on the evidence of my own eyes, that the flag was quite up to the masthead. Nor was there any more truth in the statement as to the wounded. The whole of these incidents were the shameless fictions of the Ottoman Consulate at Ragusa. W. J. S.

CHAPTER IX.

THE Turks remained quiet in Trebinje until the 29th, the road being in undisturbed possession of Peko. Muktar, stirred out of his confident slumbers at Mostar, began collecting all the disposable forces from the various fortresses, and concentrating at Trebinje for an irresistible attack on the insurgents, who held the position taken from the Turks on the 21st. Unfortunately for the insurgents, the counsels of some young Russian officers who were serving as volunteers with Peko induced him to attempt a regular defence of the entrenchments—a fatal mistake, which gave Muktar the only victory ever achieved under his personal command during the insurrection.

The generalship on both sides was bad, but on that of the Turks atrocious. Peko, whatever qualities he may possess as a partisan, had no appreciation of strategical points, and those who counselled him to offer pitched battle to the Turks on an almost level plain, opposed as he was by nearly five times his numbers, were responsible for what would have been a great disaster if the Turks had any conception of how to profit by it. The insurgents were formed across the road, holding the two hillocks fortified by the Turks in the previous affair, with a left wing at right angles to this line and parallel to the road, and no right wing whatever. The peak to the south of the road was held by Peko, that on the other side by Simonics (Bogdan), and the left wing, composed of the men of Nevesinje and Zubci, by Tripko Vukalovics, nephew of the chief of the insurrectionary forces in 1862. The whole force was about 1,700 men. The bands represented were those of Petkovics, Peko, Simonics, that of Maxime being united with Peko's for want of a chief, and those of Vukalovics and Milecivics (Gligor), though of those of Peko and Simonics only about half had descended from the Baniani and Piva districts.

The Turks moved out of Trebinje on Monday night, taking positions behind Duzi, and in the morning moved slowly down the road, the principal force being on the roadway, with flanking columns in the open plain on either side. All day was occupied in this movement of about two hours' march, and as soon as the strength of the insurgents was ascertained together with their position, the force was halted just out of rifle-shot, and bivouacked in their places. The insurgents, meanwhile, had taken up their positions without ammunition, having received none since the late battle, and waited for it to arrive on the field. Some of them had not a single cartridge ; some had three or four, and a very few, who had not been engaged in the last affair, had their full allowance. At eleven a.m. arrived ammunition enough to distribute about fifteen cartridges to each man in the line, and about two p.m. the Turks moved on, their artillery, two pieces, firing sixty shells, of which only five were sent in any known relation to the insurgents, and of these one only killed a man, a splinter of stone thrown off by it hitting him on the head. The fire of musketry was incessant, but so far over-head as to be quite harmless. The column on the

road moved in close order with great steadiness, in spite of
the insurgent fire on their dense mass, where it must have
been very deadly, up to about 150 yards, when it halted
and threw out a strong column to the left, which marched
through the plain round the hill on the south of the road.

Here appeared a curious evidence of Peko's incapacity
to comprehend strategical considerations. There was in
advance of his position a slight elevation, which the insurgents had occupied in the morning, but abandoned, to concentrate their forces in the entrenched positions. This was
about to be occupied by a body of the advancing troops;
on seeing which Peko, calling on his men to follow him,
charged up one side of the hill while the Turks were going
up the other, and met them on the summit; but, to his surprise, he found only four of his men behind him. He turned
to fly, but in the advance the Turks had got between him
and his men, and with three followers, the fourth regaining
the entrenchments, he was obliged to make a detour of
several hours' march and pass between Czarina and Drien
to get back to his camp at Vukovich, late in the day, after
the battle had been fought and lost. He was believed to
have been killed or in the hands of the Turks. His men,
without a commander and discouraged by his supposed loss,
abandoned their works as soon as the Turkish column had
begun to menace their rear, and fled precipitately across the
road, drawing with them those of Simonics, who all fell back
on the elevations to the north of the road. The left wing, in
the steadiest and most deliberate manner, fell back, keeping
up a steady fire until positions were gained which checked
pursuit, and which were those along the ridge from which I
had looked at the former affair. Behind this it will be remembered was the temporary camp; but as this was in a

most exposed position, the plain half-circling it on the east, it was abandoned as soon as the wounded had been properly cared for and the dead carried away, with the exception of four, which fell into the hands of the Turks and were beheaded.

The whole force fell back on Vukovich, and the Turks, who followed at a respectful and leisurely distance, burned the deserted village, which was, of course, abandoned by the inhabitants, with the exception of three women, who were murdered. All the villages in this section up to Vukovich were then burned, and the Turks advanced to the ridge overlooking that village, where they waited, without any attempt to accelerate the movements of the insurgents, or discommode them in any way, until the village should be evacuated, when they would burn it. It was evacuated next day after a council, in which some move was decided on; and the whole band, with the exception of the wounded and their carriers, the camp-followers, and some of the timid or weak ones who had not nerve or muscle for the new undertaking, perhaps 300 or 400 in all, leaving a solid force of about 1,200 men, who made their final preparations, received their ammunition, &c., and dined gaily at Grebci, the Turkish force waiting respectfully on the heights opposite, at about 2,000 yards' distance. At about four p.m. they filed off with cheers for unknown parts, the inhabitants of Grebci meanwhile making frantic haste to get their worldly goods across the frontier before the Turks should enter and burn the village.

The escape of Peko and his band was a real masterpiece of irregular warfare. While Muktar Pasha waited till he should ascertain the movement of the insurgents, not even daring to attack Grebci, where a score or so of men only remained, Peko reached the Trebinishitza on the Popovo plain, crossed it, and marched on Ljubinje, where he captured a provision train, and then, making a wide circular march through an entirely undefended country, passed between Bilek and Trebinje, and reached Zubci without molestation. There he was rejoined by the balance of his corps, most of whom had passed through Ragusa, or by the Lloyd steamer to Castel Nuovo.

Muktar burned all the villages along the Austrian frontier between Czarina and Grebci—eleven in number—none of them previously molested, their population going to swell the number of the refugees in Dalmatia. His movement, which had only been accomplished by a concentration of all the disposable forces in Herzegovina, had been a draught of the seine come to shore empty ; and Peko, instead of being driven over the frontier, had gone to ravage the country from which the troops had been withdrawn. The road to Ragusa was open, and the population of Trebinje preserved from starvation ; for they were so far reduced that crowds followed the army out, unable to wait till the provision train could arrive from Ragusa. But now all was to be begun over again, and another long interval of inefficiency and inactivity followed, broken by the necessity of organizing another expedition to provision Niksics, now again reduced to short allowance.

The negotiations connected with the Andrassy Note (Appendix A) now began to complicate the military position, the impotence of the Porte to conquer the insurrection having long been clear to everybody on the ground. An armistice was proposed, to enable the parties to discuss tranquilly the conditions of pacification ; but the terms proposed by the Andrassy Note were, in advance even of their official notification to the insurgent chiefs, rejected by a manifesto prepared at Sutorina, where most of the chiefs were encamped owing to the severity of the winter in the mountains, small detachments only of the various corps being kept at Duga.

Receiving information of the deliberations on February 18th, I went to Sutorina, and there saw Socica and the principal chiefs, and, learning that the reply to the Note had been prepared, requested a copy for publication. This was promised for the next day. The steamer of the next morning, however, brought Colonel Monteverde, who, on learning that a manifesto was prepared, and that I was going to get a copy for publication, galloped ahead of us to Socica's head-quarters, got possession of the document, and persuaded (as he supposed) the chiefs to renounce any anticipation of the official communication of the Note. In this, as I ascertained, Monteverde acted in obedience to official indications; and when, some days later, I received at Ragusa the copy of the manifesto promised me (Appendix B), and communicated it to the Russian Consul-General there, it was received with unmistakable demonstrations of great irritation, and strong efforts were made to induce the chiefs to disavow it; and the Russian agency published a telegram denying its authenticity (see "Times," Feb. 21st); but no threats or pressure could induce them to retract, Socica distinctly and publicly declaring that he would lose his head before he would take back a word of it. It was signed by Socica and Simonics as the voivodes of Herzegovina, and Melentie as the representative of the Church; Peko as a volunteer was not included, but gave me his assurance, as did all the others, that they agreed with Socica in repelling all overtures on the basis of the Andrassy Note. The document has a certain value under the peculiar circumstances, and as showing, when put side by side with the subsequent reply (Appendix C), the real effect of Russian influence, and the degree to which, under it, the insurgents were induced to bend their previous determinations. That Russia was anxious to terminate the affair there, is to my own mind beyond question, but there was no reason why she should require the insurgents to renounce all the benefit of their own struggles and advantages. There was a clear and easy solution of the problem offered by the subsequent propositions of the insurgents in the conference at Sutorina, and the comparison of them with the former note, shows how far the insurgents had yielded to conciliation, and what direction the Russian official influence took : the first being their independent determination ; the second, the determination under Russian persuasion.

CHAPTER X.

N the beginning of March the Turkish expedition
to relieve Niksics and Goransko being about to
start, the camp at Sutorina was broken up, and
the whole force was concentrated between Baniani and
Duga. The Turks concentrated at Gatschko, while ostenta-
tious preparations were being made at Bilek, as if the army
were to start *viâ* Rudini by the upper road to Niksics.
Selim Pasha in command at Gatschko, having neither mules
nor horses for the commercial service, the insurgents were
still more thrown off their guard, and Socica making a tour
of inspection the morning of the 6th of March, perceived to
his surprise a division of Turkish troops returning from
Goransko. They had marched the night before from
Gatschko; a thousand of them carrying sacks of flour on
their backs, had reached Goransko, and set out to return
immediately.

Sending off runners to the other corps, he threw himself,
with the two hundred men with him, across the intervening
hills, and fell on the flank of the Turkish rear-guard. Peko
with his band, about equal in strength, followed quickly,
and the home guard of Piva came up in the rear, being
by chance near at hand. The rear-guard faced about,
and had fired two rounds in platoon when the firing was

heard in front of them, other bodies of insurgents having come in on the main body. Thereupon the rear-guard, fearing to be cut off, faced about and marched rapidly forward, harassed by the insurgent fire, and speedily breaking into a run.

As the different bodies of the insurgent force heard the firing, they took up the march towards the road, falling continually on the flank of the long column with fresh men, and the troops making scarcely any resistance; but, having the road open before them, they made for Gatschko rapidly. The garrison at that fortress, hearing the firing and that it approached them, sent out another battalion with two guns to meet the fugitives and cover their retreat. These met the flying column, and were instantly enveloped by it. One gun was taken on the spot, the gunners being all cut down and the mules captured; the other, on the carriage ready to fire, was dragged by the troops along the road two or three miles at least, when, the snow being nearly middle deep, in a melting and sodden state, and the wheels being up to the axles in it, it was overtaken by the insurgents and captured.

Near Lipnik is a river, dry in the summer, like the others of Herzegovina, but then swollen so high, and so rapid as to make the ford dangerous, and here the troops huddled together in a dense mass, crowding the ford, many being carried away by the torrent and drowned, and the whole exposed to the furious onslaught of the insurgents concentrating around them. It was ten o'clock at night when the pursuit ceased, with a bright moon, and those who had succeeded in fording the river escaped to Lipnik. The loss on the Turkish side was never exactly known, but one of the Russian volunteers wrote that it was a veritable St. Bartholomew—simply butchery. The number of " heads " taken

(the nose being technically a "head") was above 800.
The Kaimakam of Goransko, who had availed himself
of the opportunity to try to return to Gatschko, was
killed, and two women of his harem were taken prisoners.
With the guns were taken four boxes of ammunition for
them. Over six hundred rifles were taken, and the ammunition in the cartridge-boxes of the men killed alone,
was over 100 cartridges per man. In the early morning
the commander at Gatschko sent out a strong column to recover the guns, and as in the night the insurgents had not
been able to collect all the rifles thrown or dropped by the
way, the Turkish troops were able to carry off many rifles and
the bodies from the part of the road nearest Lipnik; the
bones of the rest still lie along the road as far as Smeretchna,
where the fight began.

The second Muratovizza brought Muktar Pasha himself
forward again, and another and again unsuccessful attempt
to pass the Duga was made, the troops reaching Zlostop,
the first block-house in the Duga, and then, either from the
depth of the snow or inability to face the insurgents, returned to Gatschko, Simonics attacking the rear-guard as
it withdrew, and pursuing it to the Turkish lines again. In
this affair Djellaledin Pasha was wounded and lost all his
baggage, and the pursuers found 122 Turkish dead on the
line when they came to count the losses. The snow in the
pass was middle deep and melting; negotiations continued
for an armistice, which the insurgents refused to accept
from the Austrians, while the Porte forbade Muktar to open
direct negotiations with them. It was again the politic conduct of the Prince of Montenegro which postponed the
crisis by allowing Niksics to be provisioned from Montenegrin territory. There is no doubt but that Niksics must

have surrendered this time if the Prince had not aided the Porte, much against the interests of the insurrection.[1]

Orders were, however, sent to the Pasha to go to Niksics at any cost, as a question of military *amour propre* apparently, and at the same time the Prince of Montenegro undertaking to negotiate a truce which Muktar appeared to be willing to treat for, while he made all his preparations to push his provision trains through, when the insurgents, deceived by the armistice negotiations,[2] were off their guard, and mostly absent to avoid the discomforts of the mountain positions about Duga, the Pasha made a dash, and, before

[1] MR. MONSON TO THE EARL OF DERBY.

My Lord,   *Ragusa, March* 28, 1876.

Muktar Pasha, Commander-in-chief in the Herzegovina, is holding daily conferences with Baron Rodich, on the means of arranging with the insurgents a suspension of hostilities.

The Austrians seem to think that the Turks are treating the question from quite an erroneous point of view, and that, instead of talking as if they had won a succession of victories, they should be as moderate in their language as befits their want of success in recent military operations.

The difficulty seems to consist chiefly in the pretension of the Turks to have the right of sending provisions into Niksics during the truce, to which the insurgents will not consent. It would appear that Niksics is now receiving small occasional supplies of provisions from Montenegro, where it is not desired that such a catastrophe should be allowed to happen as the fall of a frontier town from starvation.

I have, &c.

(Signed)   EDMUND MONSON.

[2] During several days the most active correspondence was exchanged between Vienna, Constantinople, and Cettinje, respecting the resumption of the negotiations, of which a new truce was to be the prelude. Continuing to give proofs of his good will, the Prince of Montenegro offered spontaneously to insure the passage of the provisions for Niksics by a new route, traversing the heart of his territory, and gave orders that this transport should take place without obstacle. The Sublime Porte, through the Austrian Ambassador, gave the most favourable

the insurgents were aware of the movement, he had taken possession of positions which enabled him to move his provision trains to the fortified barrack of Presieka, garrisoned by 800 men and armed with artillery.

The insurgent chiefs at once began an attack, and sending forces to the north end of the pass, and sending off to recall the absentees, beset Muktar with an energy which almost compensated for their previous negligence.   Their entrenchments, previously prepared at the almost impregnable portion of the pass, held the Turks absolutely powerless while the forces were increasing behind them.   The position was so desperate that even at Gatschko the army was believed to be lost.   When, however, nightfall set in, the Turks remaining assurances, and Muktar on his side, declared to the Governor of Dalmatia that he was ready to conclude an armistice, provided that Niksics was provisioned.

The event has proved how deceitful were these appearances.   It is not in our province to judge of the impression which it has produced on the Powers ; but we do not fear to say aloud that we have been trifled with, and what is much more painful, that we have helped in deceiving the Herzegovinians at the very time that they had confided to us the defence of their interests.   The discussions which put them off their guard were only a feint to facilitate a second surprise ; and, it appears, it was from Constantinople itself that the formal orders went for a new attack.   This last succeeded, at least in part, in attaining its principal object, the revictualling of Niksics.   Muktar Pasha succeeded, in fact, on the 28th of April, in covering the entry of a portion of his convoy, the insurgents not finding themselves sufficiently numerous to prevent it.   The following day, and the day after, it is true, being reinforced by the arrival of several of their corps, they made him suffer considerable losses, and nearly cut off his retreat on Gatschko.   Some thousands of dead and wounded, and the provisioning of a place for a few days, are the only results of a diplomatic manœuvre, the characterizing of which we leave to the judgment of Europe.   There is as yet no appearance that the insurrection is enfeebled by it ; the Herzegovinians are, on the contrary, more animated than ever.—*Memorial of the Prince of Montenegro, May 8th.*

in their defensive positions, the insurgents retired to their
camps and lighted their fires a mile away, whereupon Muktar,
conjecturing justly the position of matters, gave orders to
move on the entrenchments, which were found completely
abandoned, and secured all the positions necessary to
protect his movements the next morning. The insurgents,
finding their strongest positions lost, contented themselves
by fighting to retard the Turkish movements, and inflict
such losses as they could. Muktar reached the entrenchments at Gatschko by a frightfully harassed retreat on the
21st, with losses amounting to 2,800 men killed and wounded.

Scarcely returned to Gatschko, the Pasha made energetic
efforts to retrieve the affair and finish the provisioning.
On the 28th, having cleverly deceived the spies of the insurgents, and collected a force of about twenty-eight battalions, with 2,000 Albanians and 3,000 other irregulars, he
made another of those rapid movements which so distinguished him above all the generals who had appeared in
Herzegovina ; and while the insurgents who were about
Niksics, waiting the arrival of provisions from Montenegro,
did not anticipate any movement for several days, suddenly
arrived at Presieka and took possession of the heights at the
exit of the pass, besides taking posession of the principal
points in the ravine.

The garrison of Niksics, with part of the population, immediately made a sortie under the protection of Muktar's
left wing, and carried into the city about 15,000 pounds of
supplies ; but Muktar, after a flying visit to Niksics, set out
on his return with the same expedition and energy which
had marked his arrival, and *the same day* left Presieka for
Gatschko. His return was harassed continually, and occupied the remainder of the 28th and 29th. The insurgents

had hoped that aid would come from Montenegro to prevent Muktar's escape, and that so the whole army would
be destroyed, but they were in this disappointed, as no
help came, and their force was totally insufficient to resist
the numbers which Muktar commanded, favoured as they
were by possession of the road. Muktar himself stated
the insurgent force at 14,000,[1] but I know from Osman
Pasha, who commanded immediately in the fight of the 18th
to the 21st and superintended the re-provisioning, subse-

[1] CONSUL HOLMES TO SIR H. ELLIOT.

(Extract.)   *Mostar, April* 20, 1876.

  I have the honour to inform your Excellency that Muktar Pasha has
returned to Gatschko, without having been able to succour Niksics. He
reported having had six encounters with the insurgents, whom he reckons
to have amounted to 7,000, aided by as many more regular Montenegrin
troops. Ali Pasha has received telegrams also from Trebinje and Ragusa
informing him that bodies of Montenegrins had marched to assist the
insurgents, so that it would appear to be certain that some thousands of
Montenegrins really did take part in the opposition offered to Muktar
Pasha, though I imagine the number of 7,000 to be exaggerated. Ali
Pasha thinks that Montenegro desires to acquire Niksics and its rich
plain ; but he says that, if she gains her object, Turkey would not be
able to retain or occupy the Duga Pass, and that the Herzegovina would,
in future, be at the mercy of the Principality. He seems to think the
pacification of the Herzegovina will not take place without war with
Montenegro, as in 1861.

SIR H. ELLIOT TO THE EARL OF DERBY.

(Extract.)   *Constantinople, April* 20, 1876.

  Upon going to the Porte this afternoon, I learnt that the Sultan was
greatly incensed by the report received from Muktar Pasha of the part
taken by Montenegro in opposing the expedition sent to the relief of
Niksics.

  His Majesty had at once ordered troops to be despatched to Scutari
with a view to the adoption of immediate operations against the Principality ; even whilst I was with the Grand Vizier an aide-de-camp
arrived from the Palace with a message reiterating His Majesty's' previous orders, and a military council was about to be held to deliberate
upon the position of things.

quently, being engaged in the whole series of operations,
that the total was not above 2,000, and that he himself reported it at from 1,500 to 2,000 to his chief in the report
which was the basis of that of Muktar, in which he also
declared that "7,000 Montenegrins openly fought with the
insurgents," who also numbered another round 7,000.
Osman Pasha assured me that he was astounded at the
magnitude of the exaggeration, but the Marshal replied
that "he had his own sources of information," and persisted
in his assertion. Osman Pasha farther said that in all that
was to be seen of the rebels, which was very little, there was
no kind of distinction to be observed ; all were dressed in
the same manner, and no one could have said whether there
were Montenegrins or not. The fight was, however, maintained until the insurgents had entirely exhausted their
ammunition.

This was, I believe, the last of the serious contests about
Duga ; the final provisioning of Niksics took place without
opposition on the 4th of May, the insurgent forces having
been withdrawn to the lower country, and an armistice was
arranged for the peace negotiation.

Meantime Baron Rodich had not succeeded in making
any impression on the refugees or the small deputation of
the chiefs, whom he had requested to meet him at Sutorina.
They distinctly declined to enter into any negotiations
having, for their starting point, the return to the *status quo*
even considerably ameliorated. Returning from Sutorina,
he met at Ragusa deputies from all the villages of that district where the Herzegovinians were quartered, and old Luka
Petkovics and Melentie on behalf of the fighting men of
the lower country. They all distinctly and unhesitatingly
refused to return to their homes to accept the Turkish pro-

tection under any other condition than that of a guarantee
of Christian troops. When menaced with having all their
supplies withdrawn, they replied that it was better to starve
in a Christian land than under the Turks. To Luka and
Melentie the Governor addressed himself with great severity,
if not violence, and especially the latter, as a Churchman,
he reproached with bringing the sins of the people on his
head. The priest replied that his conscience reproached
him more for what he had done as member of the Medjlis
of Trebinje, where he had often been compelled to sign his
name to judgments which he knew to be unjust, and take
part in transactions which were more wicked than fighting
for the freedom of his people.

CHAPTER XI.

THIS act finished, the curtain fell on inaction again for a brief interval, when another attempt was made by the Austrians to find some means of arriving at a pacification. Rodics invited the Turkish functionaries to a conference at Ragusa. The insurgent chiefs at the same time were called together at Grahovo of Montenegro, by the Montenegrin authorities, who had at this time adopted the same rigorous measures against foreign volunteers crossing their frontier, which the Austrians had initiated. It was evidently done with reluctance, but it was done, and the foreigners in Montenegro after the order, were sent back to Trieste. Ljubibratics, chased from upper Herzegovina, had crossed the Narenta with 500 men, and marching towards Livno was incautious enough to approach the frontier to receive arms, &c., which were to have been sent from the committee at Sebenico or Spalato, and halting at a village which is part Turkish and part Austrian, the commander of the district frontier guard arrested him and his staff, and sent them in custody to Spalato. The arrest was unquestionably on Turkish soil; but it answered the purpose, and the band of the insurgent chief was broken up, a fragment remaining to haunt the district, under the command of a sub-chief, Yaksics.

Both Austrian and Montenegrin Governments seemed, in fact, doing all they could to discourage the insurrection. At Niksics the latter had impeded the sending of supplies to the insurgent forces, and had made the passage of the Duga not only possible, but *facile*, to the Turks, and had consequently to suffer opprobrium from the insurgents and the insurrectionary committees, which accused it of betraying the movement; and the Russian Government most unequivocally, and as energetically as possible, put its direct pressure on the chiefs to induce them to accept the Andrassy Note, at least with certain modifications, which would still respect the suzerainty of the Porte. I suppose there can be no doubt that Russia promised to support these modifications, which were substantially embodied in the Berlin Note, but their acceptance implied an effective pacification. A truce was recognized on both sides for the upper country without the formality of an armistice; and there seemed ground to hope that a basis of pacification would be found, the more that the Turkish authorities had already promised to restore the villages, &c., of the Herzegovinians,[1] and the Russian

---

[1] CONSUL TAYLOR TO THE EARL OF DERBY.

My Lord,   *Ragusa, April* 7, 1876.

The terms offered by Ali and Wassa Pashas to the insurgents are:—

1. The refugees can within four weeks from 24th March return to their homes.

2. The refugees will be supplied with grain till harvest.

3. The rebuilding of their houses will follow at Government (Turkish) cost.

4. Those who will return will be exempt from tithes for one year, and from other taxes for two years.

5. A general amnesty for all who return within four weeks.

6. Those who, in spite of these concessions, do not return, will have their lands confiscated.

These are generous terms, but the refugees are tardy in accepting them, fearing a renewal of hostilities between the insurgents and Turks, in

Government and officials showed themselves strongly in favour of a settlement.

The meeting of the superior Turkish functionaries at Ragusa was of the highest importance in its consequences on the negotiations. The cordiality of the reception accorded to the Turks by the Austrians was in itself an indication to the bystanders and the friends of the insurrection, as well as those of the Turks, that the Austrian Government was desirous to arrive at a solution, and, in my opinion, the degree to which the Austrian officials strained their inclinations to meet the Turkish views was in itself destructive to any concessions on the part of the Porte. In place of the munificent promises of reconstruction, maintenance, and compensation, and the anxious desire to conciliate the Christians, they assumed, on the contrary, a show of complete indifference on the latter point, and on the former, made public a retractation of almost all the promises made.[1] It became clear to me, from my interview,

which case, if they return, they will, as heretofore, be again the real sufferers. I have, &c.

(Signed) J. G. TAYLOR.

---

[1] MR. MONSON TO THE EARL OF DERBY.

My Lord, *Ragusa, March* 30, 1876.

Muktar Pasha left Ragusa for Trebinje yesterday morning, and Ali Pasha started this morning for the same town.

From all that I can learn, the impression produced upon Baron Rodics by the two Pashas is that the Porte has no desire to conciliate the insurgents. Baron Rodics and General Jovanovics called on me yesterday, and said that the Proclamation issued by Wassa Effendi (of which I have not as yet the translation, having only seen it in the Slav text) contained no reference to guarantees, reforms, or anything else, except the clemency of the Sultan to those who submitted within four weeks, and the threat of confiscation of the property of those who did not. That, not only did the Pashas show no conciliatory spirit, but that a fresh massacre of seven Christians (three men and four women) had just

views with the Turkish Commissioners, that nothing was to
be hoped for from them in the way of conciliation.

From what I had heard of Wassa Effendi and Ali Pasha,
I had formed expectations of liberality and seriousness of
intention in regard to the insurrection, and the manner of
dealing with it, which were entirely dispelled by a very brief
conversation with each of them. It was not necessary to
go into a lengthy discussion of affairs with either of them to
find that either they did not know, or would not be
allowed to act on the fact if they knew it, that the insurgents were in a position to defy the Porte and its means of
making head against them, and that the dangers were
increasing in a manner which none but those wilfully blind
could fail to appreciate. If their attitude was due to a *mot
d'ordre* from Constantinople, the case was hopeless; if,
which seemed to me more likely, it was due merely to the
habit of shiftlessly waiting on events and hoping for what the

taken place in the vicinity of Bilek; and a raid across the frontier near
Trebinje had been committed within the week upon some sheep belonging to Austrian subjects, who had, however, beaten off the Turks, and
saved their property.   In the face of outrages such as these, how could
it be expected that any good could be done either with the refugees or
the insurgents ?

I saw Wassa Effendi shortly before this conversation, and he absolutely repudiated the idea that any one had the right to ask the Porte for
further guarantees, his argument being that the acceptance of Count
Andrassy's Note, and the Sultan's Proclamation of Amnesty, were
guarantees enough ; and that the Porte was entitled to claim that confidence should be reposed in the intention of the authorities to carry out
the reforms, and fulfil the promises of succour for the returned insurgents and refugees.   He declared, in the most solemn manner, that he
himself would not retain his position as President of the Reform Commission for a day if he found that he was unable to act honestly in this
sense.

I have, &c.

(Signed)   EDMUND MONSON.

Powers might do for them, it was scarcely more hopeful. To what seemed to me the crucial question, of what they were prepared to do to guarantee personal security to the refugees in case they could be induced to return to their country (homes they could not be said to have), neither of them had any better reply than that they must trust to the promises and good intentions of the Imperial Government and the protection of the Ottoman troops. In Wassa Effendi I could see nothing but a very acute specimen of those Christian functionaries whose subservience to the Mussulman authority and supremacy makes their position a mere cloak and blind, behind which the old system can be carried on a little longer. He was not able even to discuss, without losing his temper, the suggestion of removing the Ottoman troops from the country, or either of the alternative projects of disarming the Mussulmans or allowing the Christians to go armed. The insurgents were expected to lay down their arms, and return to a country garrisoned by the troops whom they had lately so disastrously defeated, while the native Mussulmans, with all the new blood-feuds on their minds, were to be still allowed to retain their arms; and he did not seem to have the slightest conception that this was not personal equality before the law, much less that it was a condition no prominent insurgent would dare to accept if he valued his tenure of life.

Wassa Effendi got angry, and abruptly broke off the discussion; and, with more hope, I went to Ali Pasha, for I have known really just and liberal Mussulmans in the Turkish service, and I had heard that he was much impressed with the difficulty of the work before him. I was disappointed both with his tone and the views which he had of the matter.

His liberality was of the same kind as Server Pasha's, and, of the two, I think I should expect more of the latter. Ali was equally glib, and even more polite, but he was far less considerate in discussion than his predecessor. He smiled and was cordial, and talked very frankly, but paid very little attention to what was said on the other side. He showed simply as an adroit fencer, on the defensive in argument, evading with great dexterity every embarrassing question, but impressing me as quite incapable of a serious view of the matter, or of conceiving of his own position that it was any other than that of one who must cover a matter which could not be defended openly.

He did not, like Wassa, lose his temper, but he assumed the same tone, and, to the same questions, made the same replies. The Sultan's proclamation was in his eyes a guarantee for all liberties and security; if the insurgents wanted anything beyond, they were likely to want, for they would not be offered any other. And when I assured him, from my personal knowledge of the people, that some decided and tangible guarantee would be required, they not considering life sufficiently assured under the old conditions to induce them to venture back, he said—Wassa had said the same—that was their affair; it was quite indifferent to the Porte whether they came back or not. Further, he said that this point had not been placed before him, and he had not given it any consideration; that it was, doubtless, before the Great Powers when they discussed the matter, but he was not aware if they had decided it to be worth making stipulations about. " Lord Derby had," he said, " had the point under consideration, and if *he* had thought it worth dwelling on, we ought to know it from himself. It had not been mentioned to him (Ali Pasha), and he did not know that anybody had thought it worth examination." With regard to the question of assistance to returning refugees, he was explicit enough; the Porte did *not* mean to reconstruct the houses destroyed—only to give facilities to the returning refugees to do so for themselves, and to give food until autumn, and nothing more.

These were the three capital points for the temptation of an exiled people. It happened in the course of the two days Ali was in Ragusa that three facts came to my knowledge which served as commentaries to the points respectively. Wassa Effendi, on leaving for Mostar, insisted on having means to begin his work with. He was assured that two millions of piastres would meet him at Mostar. After a time one million arrived from Seraïevo, all in base coin, *beshliks*, loaded on donkeys, the transport of which, I am assured, had cost 38,000 piastres, and within a few days scarcely a remnant of it was in the treasury—it had gone to pay the salaries of the starving *employés*. So much for pecuniary assistance. As to the food, the captain of the "Lloyd" Levant steamer just previously arrived assured me that he had a quantity of the grain sent by the Porte on board his ship—wretched, damaged stuff, not fit to give to horses; much of it, having lain long exposed to the weather, was actually sprouting through the sacks. As to personal security, that very week one of the Christian villages which lie under the protection of the strong place of Bilek, was entered, and seven of the inhabitants were massacred in cold blood by the protectors of the population garrisoning Bilek, who entered the town afterwards, carrying the heads of the murdered—three men and four women—on the points of their weapons. I had not heard it when I saw Ali Pasha, and could not, therefore, ask him what clever reply he had to such an argument. He would, as is usual, have simply denied it.

As I anticipated, and as I imagine Rodics himself fully expected, the conference with the Turkish delegates resulted in nothing—they resolutely declined to give any guarantee of security to the refugees beyond the firman, or any pledge either to disarm the Mussulman or allow the Christian to carry arms; and the only effects of the meeting were to paralyze the Austrian efforts to pacify; and increase the distrust and determination of the insurgents.

Hostilities were carried on in the lower country in a desultory sort of way, mostly by raiding, &c., during another month. The Austrians as a last inducement withdrew the supplies hitherto given to the families; but finding even this compulsion ineffectual to induce any one to return, revoked the withdrawal after a few days.

The final conference between Rodics and the insurgent chiefs to discuss pacification was appointed for April 5th. Prior to this meeting, however, they were met by Mr. Wesselitzky, a Russian of Herzegovinian descent who had been engaged in philanthropic labour in behalf of the refugees in Croatia and Dalmatia, and who, under the correct hypothesis that his labours had given him a certain moral influence amongst the insurgents, was requested by the Russian Government to use that influence to induce them to accept the Andrassy Note. Mr. Wesselitzky was in no other sense a Russian diplomatic agent, nor was he, as I have good reason to believe, in the confidence either of the Russian or the Montenegrin Government, or employed for any other reason than that stated, and because he was not a Russian agent in the responsible sense of the term. He was a philanthropist, with perhaps some diplomatic aspirations born of the position in which he found himself, but with no diplomatic capacities which would have induced the Russian or any other Government to repose in him any grave responsibility. He was personally opposed to the extension of the authority of the Prince of Montenegro over Herzegovina, and regarded autonomy as the most desirable solution, but no one doubted his interest in the people, owing to which he was intrusted with considerable sums of money by the Russian committees for the refugees, and later for the insurgents; he may have been also so charged by the Russian Government, but I never saw any proof of this being the case. His importance and functions were much overrated by a portion of the press, which attributes mysteries and powers to Russian intrigues far beyond what human nature would sustain. The only fact of any real importance in his connection with the insurrection is, that he was requested to advise the acceptance of the Andrassy Note, and did so.

CHAPTER XII.

THE reply of the chiefs to Rodics, who met them the day after, was to the following effect. They accepted the pacification under Turkish sovereignty under the conditions :—

1. That one-third of the land they held in lease should become the property of the Christians. (*See Note, Appendix C.*)

2. That those who returned should receive assistance to enable them to rebuild their houses and churches, provide seed, &c., and subsistence for one year, and be freed from the tithe for three years.

3. That the Turkish troops should be limited to garrisons in Niksics, Trebinje, Stolatz, Mostar, Fotcha, and Plevlie.

4. That the Christians should be allowed to retain their arms until the Mussulmans were disarmed.

5. That the chiefs should, jointly with the authorities, choose the new councils.

6. That Austria and Russia should have commissioners in the garrison towns to superintend the measures of pacification.

The Porte, so far as I could learn, never condescended to consider or reply to these propositions, which it characterized as "unheard of demands," and yet the question of

peace or war lay in their acceptance or non-acceptance.[1]
There was nothing in the conditions laid down by the chiefs
which was not reasonable and absolutely necessary to the
security of the returned population, and there was no reason
for their non-acceptance but the pride of the Turkish Government and governing class. The blind and stiff-necked
amour propre of an incapable and irrational despotism,
raised into real importance only by the less rational respect
paid it by certain of the European Governments, threw away
this new opportunity for the peaceful and gradual solution of
the question which Europe had been simmering over for fifty
years. The insurgents had been, by the united influence of

---

[1] Her Majesty's Government have been informed that the Porte has
been advised through the Turkish Ambassador at St. Petersburg to
express its readiness to examine the counter proposals of the insurgents,
in which case Prince Gortchakoff would advise the Chiefs to open communications with the Turkish authorities. As the Porte, however, is of
opinion that an assent to this suggestion would be sanctioning in some
degree Russian intervention, Cabouli Pasha has been instructed to
express the regret with which his Government have learnt that the
Governments of Austria and of Russia, after having approved as sufficient the offers of the Porte, should now recommend it to examine new
demands put forward by the insurgents, and of which the Porte has received no official communication.—*Memorandum of Sir A. Buchanan
to Andrassy*, *April* 20.

Prince Gortchakoff then entered into an explanation of his late interview with Cabouli Pasha, and of the sensation which the Pasha's telegram
relating to it had caused at Constantinople, and read a letter he had
addressed to General Ignatieff on the subject.

In that letter Prince Gortchakoff informed General Ignatieff that, on
being asked to support the advice given to the insurgent chiefs by
General Rodics, viz., to refer their counter-proposals to the Turkish
authorities, he (the Prince) had replied that he would willingly do so,
provided that he was certain that the Porte would consent to receive
those proposals, and to treat with the bearers of them. But the Porte
had declined all negotiations, and had appealed to arms.—*Augustus
Loftus to Lord Derby*, *April* 22.

Russia and Austria, brought to reduce their terms of submission to Turkish authority to the last concessions which safety and justice permitted, as will be admitted by all who know the internal condition of the Turkish provinces; and Montenegro was ready to support, with all its influence and appliances, pacification on those terms. The responsibility lies with the Porte and its advisers that this crisis, like the others, passed without result.

The news which came on the 8th of May, that Muktar was assembling forces to attack the insurgents as soon as the armistice expired, and that several battalions more had arrived at Klek, dissipated any idea of peace which might have been entertained, and the Herzegovinians went to the section of country between Baniani and Trebinje, where a desultory warfare was carried on, no feat of arms at all noteworthy being recorded. The Berlin Note, which followed the failure of the Conference at Sutorina and Ragusa, brought the action of the Powers into the principal position in the affair; and its final rejection by England, and consequent abandonment by the three Empires, brought matters to a crisis, from which there was no escaping without a war. The Porte was utterly unable to suppress the insurrection, and the Pashas accused the Prince of Montenegro of sheltering the insurgents when beaten and allowing them to recruit their forces and strength in his territory, and return; though the fact is, that in no case had the Turks been able to drive a single insurgent across the frontier, or even to approach it. On the other hand, the violent menace against the principality, reinforcing his own tendencies, induced the Prince to undertake at Berlin and with the friendly Powers, to protect the interests of the insurgents diplomatically, and, in consequence, they formally put themselves entirely under his guidance, and established obligations which made it impossible for him to withdraw the moral and even the military support which had hitherto been permitted or accorded. The Prince, in his memorial, stated these considerations fairly, and, I think, accurately, though in justice I must say, that that document is not as veracious in its statement of what had been done at an earlier period to prevent aid reaching the insurgents.[1]

But the position was a trying one for the principality. To withdraw was impossible in the actual temper of the people; for although in diplomatic calculations a people always does what the Government says must be done, we find in actual practice that the strongest Governments have *sometimes* to take account of public opinion, even where there is a good police and standing armies. To use efforts to suppress the insurrection without any substantial concession on the part of the Porte was quite out of the question; to endure the burden and expense of the actual condition was to invite ruin;[2] to expel the refugees impossible, and I am satisfied

---

[1] " He has assured himself of the numbers of those who have disobeyed him (two or three hundred), and punished each of them with the utmost rigour of the law."—*Memorial, &c.* It is safe to say that no one was punished.

[2] This struggle, perpetually renewed, places Montenegro in an intolerable position, which its Sovereign submits pressingly to the urgent and serious consideration of the Great Powers.

His subjects, habituated as they are to obey the laws, cannot forget that the Herzegovinians are their brothers in race and religion; that they are, in fact, a part of the same nation, divided by a line of demarcation merely political. The recent history of the most civilized nations shows that with the best organized means of action great Governments may find themselves powerless long to restrain the explosion of overexcited national sentiment.

To preserve order they have been obliged, willingly or unwillingly, to yield to the current of public opinion, and yet such opinion has been

that the public opinion of any liberal and enlightened country, without interest in the question, would applaud the course the Prince actually followed.

To add to the stringency of the position, the Turks massed large numbers of troops on the southern frontier of Montenegro, and blockaded the whole line. The Prince

nowhere exasperated by the spectacle of horrors and devastations such as those of which Montenegro is, so to say, the ocular witness.

Her territory is full of refugee families, whose dwellings have been destroyed, and whose means of living have been annihilated. Such a state of misery must have been seen to be imagined. The charity of Europe and the generosity of the Emperors of Austria and Russia have powerfully contributed to the maintenance of these unfortunate beings, but the heaviest part of this daily work none the less falls to the charge of Montenegro. This people, small and poor, shares what it has with the exiles, whose number, already nearly equal to half its own, seems to increase every day. What it does, it does heartily and without regret ; but the moment approaches when it will be materially incapable of doing anything ; it will have nothing left to share.

The very configuration of our frontiers, badly defined and irregular, is an inevitable source of conflicts, the possible gravity of which, under present circumstances, cannot be ignored.

Again, the Christian villages in the Herzegovinian districts of Piva, Baniani, Gatschko, and Zubci, whose situation places them outside the zone occupied by the Turkish troops, shelter a population of refugee families like that which has fled to us, equally deprived of all, and maintained more or less well by the same resources. The movements in advance of the Ottoman army menace these localities ; now, occupation by it simply means pillage, fire, and massacre, above all since it has been reinforced by Arabs and Bashi-bazooks, whose reputation for want of discipline and for ferocity is nothing new. Quite recently, for example, the Albanian irregulars turned out of their road to sack and fire the Christian village of Golia. Europe does not certainly expect us to allow such ravages to be committed at our very gates without trying to prevent them.

These are only a few of the points of the situation as it presents itself from the Herzegovinian side ; they are certainly sufficient to inspire the most serious apprehensions. They only represent, however, a part of the dangers which menace peace.—*Memorial, &c.*

had, from various motives, strongly discouraged any insurrection on that side, and, except as a menace to him, there
was no object in the gathering of troops at Scutari and
Podgoritza.

The murders at Salonica, the affairs of Bulgaria, and the
consequent confusion of Turkish affairs may well serve as
excuse for the absolute paralysis which prevailed in Herzegovina through May and June, the troops only massing at
Gatschko, as if to menace to enter Montenegro *viâ* Niksics
The insurgents were concentrated mainly at Baniani, with
some flying bands in the plain and towards Stolatz, and only
unimportant raids broke the monotony of the situation. It
was evident that the time was rapidly approaching when the
character of the struggle was to change. The Russian influence on Cettinje (I can say nothing of Servia), in place of
being a restraining one as before, became a neutral one ;
and though the Prince was clearly informed that he had no
territorial advantages to gain by going to war, and had no
ground to hope for aid from Russia in such a contingency,
he was left free to act as he saw fit, bearing the entire
responsibility of his actions ; and I have what I consider
most reliable assurances that to the final councils and decisions the Czar was absolutely a stranger.

But that there might be no doubt that Turkey was preparing to attack Montenegro, the Kutchi, a Serb tribe in
Upper Albania, conterminous with the Berdas, were summoned to find hostages to keep the peace, and submit to
the Turks. The Kutchi are closely akin to the Montenegrins, and were, before the last boundary commission put
them beyond it, within the frontier, but have never accepted
Turkish functionaries, though the Turks held a fortress, that
of Medun, in their territory, and early in the spring several

of the chiefs had been made prisoners by the Turks as they
came to the bazaar at Podgoritza and carried to Scutari,
but were afterwards released, and nothing more was
attempted for the moment in that direction.   In the latter
part of June the new requisition to the tribe to send in hostages for good behaviour excited the most determined opposition.   The Kutchi in themselves were entirely unobnoxious
to the Turkish Government, and were a peaceful people;
but their kindred with the Montenegrins, and the position
of their country, which stands on a great flanking bastion to
the plain of Bjelopawlitje, which, it will be remembered,
nearly divides Montenegro, and leads to Niksics, were strong
reasons for securing the submission of the tribe, and the road
through their country, before attacking Montenegro: and the
large concentration of troops at Podgoritza was opposed by
two battalions at Rogami.

The insurrection, as such, had in the latter part of June
assumed the quiet of a chrysalis about to burst its old
envelope and spread its wings.   Servia was (as she supposed) preparing for war, and Montenegro had completed
her simple armament by the addition of 6,000 old breech-
loaders and some hundred thousand cartridges.   Half the
fighting force of the principality was on the frontier when I
again reached there in the last days of June, 1876.

I found the same doubts, and hopes, and fears at work
as when I was there a year before.   Nobody believed in
Servia, and yet she had promised to declare war: the Prince
himself felt confident, such were the obligations entered into,
that the sister (and rival) principality could no longer
refrain, and my own information leads me to believe that a
revolution in Servia would have followed a definite refusal
to declare war on the Porte.

The declaration of war struck me as impolitic. Supposing war intended, the actual position was ruinous to Turkey, and by relaxing a little further the restrictions of the previous policy, a larger outlet to the popular agitation would have been provided, and the Porte driven into a critical condition from which it could only liberate itself by concessions or provoking the catastrophe which Europe deprecated. The Prince had only to relax his restraints to send ten thousand men across the frontier; and if the Porte saw fit to declare war, the responsibility would have been on it. The declaration of war, though less politic, was more in accordance with the temperament of the Prince and his people, and at the same time more honourable; and the popular feeling was such that there was no trifling with it. If Servia had declared war, and Montenegro had not followed instantly, the Prince of Montenegro must have abdicated. If the voice of the people be not the voice of God, it is sometimes the voice of destiny, which, as a general thing, is the only form that Governments recognize Him in; and Fate spoke on that day, July 2nd, when the fires so long smouldering burst out into open conflagration, and the last word was said of the insurrection in Herzegovina, which disappears in the war between Turkey and the Principalities.

The last act of the insurrection, through the fatal blundering of the Porte, coincided with the first of the war, by the attack on the Kutchi on July 1st, resulting in the first battle of Medun, in which the Turks were disastrously defeated and Medun placed under the blockade, which resulted, after many fruitless attempts to relieve it, in its surrender some months later, most of the fighting and unparalleled disasters

L

to the Turkish army on the southern frontier arising from this faithless and needless war against an indomitable but inoffensive shepherd tribe. It may be said that the Porte began the war by an act of aggression and supreme injustice.

CHAPTER XIII.

WHILE these words are being written, the consequences of that war are still pending, and all
Europe is watching the solution of the grave
difficulties involved, hoping that that solution may be a final
one. To be such it must be radical; and it appears to me
that the proper way of arriving at the solution in the general
interest, is to lay aside for the moment all the particular interests, and begin with the vital element in the question.

This is the demonstrated incapacity of the Ottoman
Government to secure the conditions of progress or even
favourable existence to its subjects. The reason of that incapacity is in the *raison d'être* of the government—the right
to govern without a reciprocal obligation to protect—a right
inherent in the true believer to dispose, without any restric-
tion, of the earth and all that is on it, without any other
obligation than such as the Koran contains, and the Koran
recognizes no obligation towards an infidel other than that
of a master to a slave. It is the nature of this sacred right,
which no temporal combination or convention can impugn,
which throws the Mussulman out of the comity of Christian nations, and makes his government in its very inception
a relation of owner and rayah (or herd).

We are not obliged to go to Mohammedanism to learn

that while men readily accept all the license any religion may give them, they are slow to accept the self-denial which may be coupled with it in the precept : it is not surprising that while Mussulmans universally claim the privileges of their faith, there should be very few who accept the finer virtues which the Koran may point out.   The fact is, that the Mussulman has always held, and still holds, his power and dominion *as Mussulman*, and whatever theory may suggest, practice demonstrates that that dominion is, in Europe at least, an evil mitigated only by entirely alien interests ; as between the ruler and the ruled in Turkey, there is no mitigating relation. The Turkish Government is bad mainly because it is a Mussulman Government, and because, with such a people, a Mussulman Government must, in all probability, necessarily be bad.   It is an intolerable slavery, in all respects as bad, and in some much worse, than American black slavery was.   The only good that the governed derive from it is that they sometimes arrive at the patience and rest of the martyrs.

The only cure for it is, that it should cease to be Mussulman—and this is equivalent to its ceasing to exist.   It is impossible to reform it, because the very principle of its organization must be changed to admit any reform.   The men who constitute the Government hold their places not because of their fitness, but because they are Mussulmans ; and while this principle is admitted the better elements of the population are excluded from any share in government. It will be useless to insist on this Mussulman caste admitting the Christian to equal rights ; and those who regard this as a possible solution have studied carelessly history and human nature. We may find an individual sovereign capable of an abdication of his rights for the general good; but that a caste should voluntarily abandon its privilege does not come within human probabilities. The difficulty of it may be conceived by supposing that the people of England three hundred years ago had been called on to admit Jews to the fullest privileges of citizenship,—nobility, legislation, the bench—and all at once. Yet this would have been a trifle compared with what is demanded of the Turk, because at best the Jews would have been a small minority in England, while the Mussulman reformer must admit an immense majority, which, *as majority*, must rule him. A nearer illustration would have been to suppose that in the year 1860 the population of the Southern American States should have been called on to admit the negro population to civic rights and equal privileges with the whites. Is it conceivable that, with all their higher civilization, the caste of masters would have yielded to any other consideration than force? On what basis can we found a supposition that the more ignorant, fanatical Mussulman, lifted by both caste and creed into rule, shall abdicate under persuasion, or, if compelled by greater force, will not look for his opportunity to conspire and revolt against this usurping lower caste? Is it not clear, then, that equality in self-government is merely bottling up anarchy in the empire? Is it more, indeed, than a substitution of a two-handed anarchy for the one-handed which now exists? Is it not clear that this caste government will neither abdicate voluntarily nor submit patiently to deposition? It is a system which theory and practice alike indicate as an utterly inflexible one—an old bottle which will not hold a new wine. For five centuries it has not changed, except for the worse, in the midst of Governments everywhere changing for the better, and races growing wiser and stronger. Should it grow so weak as to fall under the

control of another Government, it will but be the auto-
maton whose wires shall be the intrigues of the nearest, the
most interested, and most crafty.

The interests of civilization—of Europe entire—demand
its replacement by a new Government, which shall be amen-
able to those interests and to progress, and which shall at
least prepare for a permanent one ; and the greatest security
for that common amenableness is that all Europe shall
participate actively in its foundation and watch over its development.   The religious question must be treated with the
utmost toleration ; but the interests of everybody concerned
demand that toleration should not be extended to cover
intolerance, especially in favour of a creed essentially de-
grading and antagonistic to progress.   There is no sound
reason, political, religious, or social, for the preservation of
the Mussulman empire, and many for its overthrow—no
difficulty in the solution of the problem could it be attacked
by united Europe.

" Yes," it is said, " but with what shall we replace it ? "

It seems to me in the highest degree probable that having
once admitted the necessity for its cessation, we shall more
quickly find an accord over the manner of replacing it. It is
in attempting to reform it that the danger lies ; and I feel
strongly that once Europe is agreed to abolish the Mussulman Government in the European provinces, the common
sense and common interest of Europe will find a solution
which shall definitely avert what is, after continuance of
that Government, the worst thing which could happen—an
European war on this question.

It is universally asserted that the Turk, in his popular
character, is an excellent creature. Let us believe, then, that
he will be a submissive and orderly subject, as excellent

people always are—we shall have no trouble from him. The Pashas are mostly ignorant or corrupt, or both (with exceptions, mainly of renegades), and the mass of the Christian employés are even less trustworthy for any purposes of reconstruction. Foreign administrators are the only agents capable of commanding the respect of all classes, and the only conceivable material with which to fill the void made by the banishment of the Pashas and Effendis; and while Europe may well be governed by diplomatic considerations in choosing the responsible heads of the new Government or Governments (in which the most disastrous error would be the choice of some incapable younger son to be the mask of intrigues and the shelter of new forms of Byzantinism), it is but common sense to insist that the local administrators should be those who know the people, their ways, and language. Self-government, in the sense in which it has been given to Greece and Servia, is as impracticable to the Rayah now, as it was disastrous to the Rayah of those States. The freed slave is not fit to be at once master even of himself. The less change made in the condition of the Bulgarian or Bosniak the better; and the least change from a bad despotism is that to a beneficent one. The experience of Greece and Servia proves most conclusively that the too-quick transition from despotism to popular self-government (even to the former, which by all its popular instincts is democratic) has been a disastrous boon—has proved mainly the source of political intrigue and corruption; and the Slav, whose character is more in sympathy with patriarchal than popular institutions, can at once be more easily led and less safely loosed than even the Greek.

The capital error in Europe was the not aiding and encouraging the Turkish provinces to rise entirely and

simultaneously, and helping them even, if necessary, in their
self-liberation as she has helped the Turks, with arms and
means, leaving the discipline of war and military organization to establish the bases of political organization. The
process would have been costly, but would have been
profitable in the end; for it would have made of these
slaves, men, as it has, to a certain extent, done in Herzegovina and Bosnia—would have brought forward their
natural chiefs and established a moral authority of the
highest importance in the new state of things. War and
death are not so dreadful as slavery and corruption ; and it
remains to be seen if the solution to be adopted will not in
the end cost more bloodshed than the natural solution by a
general insurrection.

   That solution, from which the timid conservatism of the
day revolts, would have obviated the great present difficulty
of "who shall reorganize?" by allowing the organization to
take its natural bent. Liberty has not always had a nursing-
mother, and the nations which profit most by their freedom have earned it by sacrifice and voluntary subjection.
Analogy allows us to suppose that the condition of Bosnia
under complete autonomy would be worse than that of
Servia, since the latter did substantially organize herself,
just as Servia is in a worse state politically than Montenegro,
because the latter again completed its organization entirely
in accordance with the habits of its people. The less
foreign interference (and the less alien the interferer) in such a
process the better, whether of institution or individuals, and
therefore Eastern ways are safer to trust than Western, since
the representative system, to which the West has grown
habituated, is the worst possible for the present condition
of the East. The more personal the new Government there-

fore the better (even Servia and Greece I believe to be
more injured than benefited by their popular representations
and legislatures, and I make no question that for any people
escaped from such a bondage a mild despotism is the only
safe agent for reorganization), and for the Slav the work of
personal government is both more useful and more easily
applicable.

So far as Bosnia and Herzegovina are concerned, there
could be no better administrators than some of the Austrian Slav military commanders—particularly Rodics and
Ivanovics ; and no better system than that of the military
frontiers—the self-respect and subordination of military
discipline being elements of primary importance to these
people ; and I can conceive no permanent bettering of these
provinces, which shall not unite them under one organization
with Dalmatia, except such part as may be wisely united to
Montenegro.

What difference may exist between Bulgaria and those
provinces I cannot indicate. I have never perceived, however, any great difference between the Rayahs of different
race—whatever may be the original character, the burden
of its slavery leaves it but one shape—that which its bitter
necessity and narrow range of life enable it to preserve, and
this is everywhere nearly the same, the same vices, the same
virtues, with a difference of a greater or less capacity of
enduring before revolting.

I believe that the truest and least dangerous or costly
solution would be in the participation of England with
Russia, and the utilizing of the unequalled experience in
such work of English Indian administrators, which, judging
from my own experience, would give a confidence to the
populations such as I do not believe Russian administrators

alone are likely to enjoy ; but failing that, there is nothing
but Russian or Austrian for every responsible position.

The Mussulman as a material for this purpose is mere dead
bone, and must be eliminated. There is no man of the
ruling class capable of the radical change *in habit of ruling*
which is necessary—none so liberal that all the prejudices
of a lifetime will not fail to prevent his adoption of a new
and radically different manner of looking at his duties.
His political education is based on the inherent right to
govern according to his own pleasure and judgment. Subordination of the governor to legislation never enters into the
conception of one of his race, not even those who have the
dubious advantage of European education. The absolute
extirpation of Mussulman heads of administration—bag and
baggage if needs be—is the essential basis of reorganization, and total disarmament the next most imperious
necessity.

The substitution of foreigners as heads of provincial and,
to a certain extent, of local administration, appears to me
the imperative *first* step, if future dangers and changes are to
be avoided ; but the existing order of things contains much
that is good, with strong conservative restraints on the person which should not be withdrawn too rapidly if society is
not to be utterly disorganized. I conceive that the old forms
should be preserved for the present, and the substitution of
the lowest class of functionaries with whom the population
come into habitual and direct contact, and on whom depends, in a great degree, the order of social existence,
carried on by degrees. I would keep (if a peaceful solution
of the problem is still practicable) this lower organization as
it is, and the *personnel* as far as possible, retaining the
mechanism, and only rejecting piece by piece the old

material as it may be found unworthy. The retention of a Mussulman Kadi in his place, when he is a just man, would disarm all Mussulman apprehensions, while the substitution of a Christian, whenever the old one is found to be unjust, would conciliate the Christian with the system and with the Mussulman population.

But the social organization of the Slav is essentially a family confederation ; and adherence to this system will rapidly restore the proper restraints of authority, while the natural separation which it would bring about between the Christian and Mussulman communities would obviate any occasion for hostility between the two. In this system the minor differences between members of the same community are judged by the head of the great family, who holds patri-archal authority over the whole clan, as we should call it. This system, at least, should prevail in Bosnia and Herze-govina.

The condition of Montenegro shows the normal organiza-tion of a Slav population, and so far as the authority of the Prince of Montenegro will reach, no better settlement could be made than its establishment. That the system is suc-cessful is seen by the fact that all round the actual territory of Montenegro the Prince is recognized as actual political head ; and I have myself heard Turkish functionaries in Albania praise his justice and trustworthiness in terms which recalled Haroun al Raschid, while in any dispute in which Turk and Christian are engaged near the frontier, and in which the Turk believes he is in the right, the disputants go to a Montenegrin judge in preference to a Turkish one.

This proves not only that the system of a patriarchal despotism suits the people we have to deal with, but that the question of a cordial co-existence of the Turk and the

Christian is not one which need cause any difficulty. The Turk who has passed his life in the enjoyment of privileges inconsistent with the rights of the subject people, will not be able to submit to the change ; but the men of the Mussulman population will not only submit to any fair government, but will be in every way bettered by the change. That this will be the case is confirmed to me by the opinions of the most experienced foreign residents I met in or about Herzegovina. But any attempt to introduce representative government, dependent on a system of more or less universal suffrage, will certainly develop an anarchy only less injurious than the system which now exists. Experience in popular government shows that with the ignorant, even when long time emancipated, the possession of political power, far from developing personal liberty, throws the whole power into the hands of the professed politician, the demagogue, or the conspirator. The power of choosing any of their rulers given to the Rayahs, ignorant of everything but the oppression of government, may well be considered a doubtful boon ; the extension of that power beyond those lower functionaries above mentioned, whose office and qualifications the people can comprehend, would be preparing the ground for an anarchy which will offer the opportunity to the most insidious of the plans which (I believe unjustly) are attributed to Russia. I should fear the Czar—*dona ferentem* —offering constitutional government, more than carrying out a military occupation, which would in time breed rebellion and animosity, and weaken rather than strengthen his position.

But whatever may be the solution which the wisdom, or the fears, of Europe shall impose, there is nothing, I must repeat, but disaster, to be hoped for from compromise with

the question of Ottoman Administrators. If in the *débris* of
the breaking-up ship of state there be a few planks of sound
material, experience only can tell with certainty; but in any
case the preservation even of the smallest part of the administration, local or general, *in a position of responsibility towards
the Sublime Porte* will be but the patching a new coat with
old cloth; the covering up of embers for future conflagration; and the most of all to be apprehended is the appointment of the Christian governors bred by the Porte, adroit in
all the arts of the courtier, but tried in none of the virtues
of good government, whose career has been made by
sycophancy and betrayal of their co-religionists, by being
more Turk than the Turk himself, and by prostituting a
greater talent and higher political capacities to the support
of a misgovernment which would have perished long ago
but for them. Wherever we may look for the fidelity and
uprightness needed in the heads of administration, we shall
assuredly not find it in the time-serving Christian Pasha
who has won his grade only by a devotion to the profitable
barbarism which "out-herods Herod," and leaves but one
doubt—whether he was ever capable of fidelity even to his
Mohammedan master. These men can only serve Europe
well when there is no interest but that of Europe to enlist
their devotion; and as long as any trace of responsibility to
the old condition of things remains, no material can be so
untrustworthy to reconstruct with as this; and what is,
perhaps, of more immediate consequence, there is no one in
whom the Rayah has so little confidence, or for whom he
has so profound a hatred. There is not a province in the
Turkish empire, probably, which if left to choose would not
prefer a Turk as governor to any Christians in the Turkish
service. The latter are recommended neither by the

popular nor the European interest, and the only motive for retaining them would be to compromise with an interest whose utter exclusion from the administration is the *sine quâ non* of a final settlement.   England cannot safely leave her interests in the hands of a class whose whole success has been of that kind which a healthy and energetic national exis-tence would speedily eliminate—a fungoid parasitic growth which may be ornamental, but is more likely to be fatal. Whatever the interests of England may be, let Englishmen look after them; but I would sooner trust them to the Russian than the Levantine, should the contingency arise which demands a choice between the two.   England can afford to be generous,—she cannot risk a chance of betrayal at a point where she has nothing to fear from open force, but everything from intrigue.

APPENDIX A.

THE ANDRASSY NOTE.

Buda-Pest, December 30, 1875.

INCE the commencement of the troubles in the Herzegovina, the European Cabinets interested in the general peace have been compelled to fix their attention on the occurrences which threatened to endanger it.

The three Courts of Austria-Hungary, Russia, and Germany, after exchanging their views on this subject, have united for the purpose of employing in common their efforts for pacification.

This object appeared too much in conformity with the general wish for them to doubt that the other Cabinets, when invited to associate themselves in the movement through their Representatives at Constantinople, would hasten to join their efforts to ours.

The Powers have come to an agreement to make use of all the influence at their disposal in order to localize the conflict, and diminish its dangers and calamities by preventing Servia and Montenegro from participating in the movement.

Their language has been the more effectual from being identic, and has, consequently, testified the firm determination of Europe not to permit the general peace to be imperilled by rash impulses.

The Cabinets, moreover, have offered to the Turkish Government the good offices of their Consular Agents to assist in putting an end to the insurrection. In the pursuit of this object, they have been equally careful to avoid all meddling, and to guard the dignity, rights, and authority of the Sovereign.

The Delegates were not authorized to constitute themselves a

Commission of Inquiry, or to make themselves the advocates of the wishes of the insurgent populations. Their mission was to undeceive them as to any assistance to be expected from without, and to exhort them to disperse after setting forth their wishes and grievances. The Powers merely reserved the power of urging on the Turkish Government such of the demands of the insurgents as should appear to be legitimate. This conciliatory action of the Cabinets sufficiently testified to the friendly intention which had inspired their good offices. It showed that in their eyes there existed a complete identity in the interests of Europe, of the Porte, and of the insurgent populations, to put an end to a ruinous and sanguinary conflict, and to prevent its recurrence by serious reforms and effective improvements of a nature to reconcile the real necessities of the country with the legitimate requirements of authority.

Such is briefly the history of the proceedings of the Powers since the outbreak of the insurrection.

The Cabinets have till now been especially guided by the desire to avoid everything that could be construed as an unseasonable interference on the part of Europe.

Accordingly all the Cabinets have confined themselves to recommending the Sultan not to trust solely to military measures, but to apply himself to combating the evil by moral means, with a view to avert future disturbances.

In acting thus, the Cabinets intended to furnish the Sublime Porte with the moral support of which it stood in need ; and, further, to give it time to pacify feelings in the revolted provinces, hoping that all danger of ulterior complications might thus be averted.

Unfortunately their hopes have been disappointed. On the one hand, the reforms published by the Porte do not appear to have had in view the pacification of the populations of the insurgent provinces, or to be sufficient for the attainment of this essential object. On the other hand, the Turkish arms have not been successful in putting an end to the insurrection.

Under these circumstances, we think that the moment has arrived for the Powers to agree on a course to be pursued in common, to prevent the peace of Europe being ultimately compromised by a continuation of the movement.

In common with the other Powers, we have applauded the benevolent intentions which have inspired the recent manifestoes of the Sultan. The Iradé of October 2, and Firman of December 12, contain a series of principles intended to introduce reforms into the organization of the Ottoman Empire. There is reason to believe that these principles, if embodied in wisely-conceived legislative measures, and if, above all, their execution fully corresponds with the enlightened views which have dictated them, will introduce real ameliorations into the administration of Turkey.

We cannot, however, disguise from ourselves that the projected reforms cannot, by themselves, arrest, even momentarily, the shedding of blood in the Herzegovina and Bosnia, still less establish on a secure basis the future tranquillity of these portions of the Ottoman Empire.

In fact, on examination of the contents of the Iradé of October 2 and the Firman of December 12, one must acknowledge that the Sublime Porte appears to be engrossed rather with general principles which, when they have been formulated, will serve as bases for the administration of the Empire, than with the pacification of the provinces at present in revolt.

Now it is for the interest of the Ottoman Government that peace should, above all, be assured ; for, so long as it is unsecured, it will be impossible to carry out even the principles which the Porte has proclaimed.

On the other hand, the state of anarchy which prevails in the provinces to the north-west of Turkey not only involves difficulties for the Sublime Porte, but also conceals grave danger to the general tranquillity ; and the different European States cannot see with indifference the continuation and aggravation of a state of affairs which already weighs heavily on commerce and industry, and which, by daily shaking more and more the public confidence in the preservation of peace, tends to compromise the interests of all parties.

We, therefore, believe that we are fulfilling an imperative duty in calling the serious attention of the Guaranteeing Powers to the necessity of counselling the Sublime Porte to complete its undertaking by such measures as appear indispensable for the re-establishment of order and tranquillity in the provinces now ravaged by the scourge of civil war.

After a confidential exchange of ideas, which has taken place between ourselves and the Cabinets of St. Petersburg and Berlin, it has been recognized that such measures must be

M

sought for in a twofold direction—first, on a moral, and secondly, on a material ground.

In fact, the material condition itself of the Christian inhabitants of Bosnia and the Herzegovina is primarily due to their social and moral position.

In examining the fundamental causes of the painful situation in which Herzegovina and Bosnia have been struggling for so many years, one is at once struck with the sentiments of enmity and rancour which animate the Christian and Mohammedan inhabitants against each other. It is this frame of mind which has rendered it impossible for our delegates to persuade the Christians that the Turkish authorities could be sincerely disposed to redress their grievances. Perhaps there is no district of European Turkey where the antagonism which exists between the Cross and the Crescent takes such an acrimonious form. This fanatical hatred and distrust must be attributed to the proximity of populations of the same race in full enjoyment of that religious liberty of which the Herzegovinian and Bosnian Christians see themselves deprived. The effect of the incessant comparison is that they feel oppressed under the yoke of a real servitude, that the very name of rayah appears to place them in a position morally inferior to that of their neighbours, and that, in one word, they feel themselves slaves.

More than once Europe has had to occupy herself with their complaints, and with the methods for terminating them. The Hatti-Humayoum of 1856 is one of the results of the solicitude of the Powers. But, even by the terms of this Act, religious liberty is still limited by clauses which, especially in Bosnia and Herzegovina, are enforced with a rigour which every year provokes new conflicts. The erection of buildings for religious and educational purposes, the use of bells, and the constitution of religious communities are still subjected in these provinces to restrictions which appear to the Christians as so many tokens always before their eyes of that war of conquest which makes them see in the Mussulmans only the enemies of their faith, and perpetuates the impression that they live under the yoke of a slavery that it is their right and their duty to shake off.

The last Firman certainly touches this point of liberty of religion, as indeed the Hatti-Chérif of 1839, the Hatti-Houmayoum of 1856, and other Acts emanating from the Sublime Porte, had already done. It confirms the powers with which the patriarchs and other spiritual heads are invested for the affairs of their respective communities and the free exercise of their religions ; but it assigns to them "as limitations the rights and authorizations which have been accorded to them." It promises also facilities for the construction of churches and schools—a promise which has been more than once notified in official documents, but which cannot be reassuring, because its realization depends on provincial authorities, who, being exposed to local pressure, could not even carry them into execution, unless the principle be clearly laid down.

The Firman, then, which has just been promulgated, goes no farther than what has already been accorded by the Hatti-Houmayoum, which, as I have already made apparent, surrounds religious liberty with restrictions which, during the last few years, have provoked numerous conflicts. With such restrictions, the concessions in question have always been insufficient to content the Christians. All the more will this be the case now, after the events which have happened to lacerate the country, and which have only envenomed the antagonism which separates the two creeds: the insurrection once suppressed, the Mohammedan element considering itself as conqueror, will doubtless seek to avenge upon the Christians the losses to which so severe a contest has subjected it. A state of affairs which should render possible the co-existence of populations who have just been fighting with so much fury, can only be assured if the Christian religion be placed in law and in fact on a complete footing of equality with Islamism, and be openly recognized and respected, and not merely tolerated, as it is at present. For this reason, as it appears to us, the guaranteeing Powers ought not only to demand of the Porte, but obtain from it as the first and principal concession, full and complete religious liberty.

Equality before the law is a principle expressly proclaimed in the Hatti-Houmayoum, and sanctioned by legislation. Doubtless it is for this reason that the recent decrees of the Sultan have omitted to mention it.

But, whilst legally obligatory, this principle is not yet generally applied throughout the Empire. As a matter of fact, the evidence of Christians against Mussulmans is received by the tribunals of Constantinople, and the majority of the large towns ; but in some distant provinces, such as Herzegovina and Bosnia, the judges refuse to recognize its validity. It would be important, then, to take practical steps to relieve the Christians in future from the fear of a denial of justice.

Another point which calls for prompt remedy is the farming of taxes. Already the Hatti-Chérif of 1839, in speaking of this system, has expressed itself in the following terms :—

" A deplorable practice still subsists, though its consequences cannot fail to be disastrous ; it is that of the venal concessions known under the name of Iltizan. By this system the civil and financial administration of a district is handed over to the will of an individual, that is to say, sometimes to the iron hand of the most violent and avaricious passions."

And the Hatti-Houmayoum of 1856 contains the following:—

" The promptest and most energetic measures will be taken into consideration for correcting the abuses in the collection of the taxes, especially of the tithes. The system of direct collection will be substituted by degrees, and as speedily as possible, for the practice of farming in all the branches of the State revenue."

In spite of these formal declarations, the system of farming is still in force to its fullest extent.

The Sublime Porte now foreshadows reforms in this direction, but without stating anything definitely. The Firman of December 12th again styles as abnormal the system for the collection of taxes actually in force. It orders the search for a mode of unification of taxes. It further prescribes measures to be taken " to prevent arbitrary proceedings in the collection of the tithe by the intervention of farmers," but it does not abolish farming.

If it is desired, then, to deprive the insurrection of an essential and perpetual source of nourishment, one of the points which must be demanded of the Porte is that she should clearly and categorically declare that the system of farming the taxes is suppressed, not only in law but in practice, for Bosnia and Herzegovina, and this measure must be immediately applied.

One of the causes which still further materially aggravate the burden, already so heavy, of the taxes in Bosnia and the Herzegovina, is that the inhabitants believe themselves to be overburdened financially for the benefit of the capital. They entertain the belief that the proceeds of the taxes are not devoted to meeting the necessities of the province, but that the total of the sum received is immediately sent to Constantinople for the use of the Central Government.

It would then be necessary to alleviate morally the weight of the burdens the province has to support, by securing that, without any encroachment on that which the expenses of the Empire require, a portion of the product of the taxes paid by the province may be reserved for purposes beneficial to its peculiar interests.

With this view, the Porte should declare that the revenue from indirect taxation should, as heretofore, be applied to the necessities of the Empire in general, but that the funds arising from direct taxation should remain in the province, and be exclusively applied in its interests to enlarge its resources and augment its prosperity.

The execution of this regulation should be placed under the control of the Elective Council, of which mention will be made in the course of this paper.

The unhappy condition of the Bosnian and Herzegovinian Christians is caused in great measure by the nature of the relations subsisting between the rural population and the landowners. Agrarian difficulties have always had a peculiarly bitter character in the countries where the landlord class differs, either in religion or nationality, from the bulk of the labourers. There are but too many examples of the furious conflicts which have resulted from such a situation.

In the provinces we are dealing with nearly the whole of the properties not belonging to the State or to the Mosques are in the hands of Mussulmans, whilst the agricultural class is composed of Christians of both creeds. The agricultural question is then complicated by religious antagonism.

After the suppression of the first insurrection of the Bosnian Beys in 1851, slavery was abolished ; but, as often happens in such cases, this measure, instead of alleviating the condition of the peasants, has only aggravated it. They are no longer treated with the same consideration as before. Now-a-days there are only two antagonistic interests, and two religions face to face. From the moment when the disappearance of the feudal system effected the transformation of the former serfs into farmers (or "métayers"), the outrageous practices of the landlords provoked numerous general or partial outbreaks. A movement of this kind having broken out in 1858 in the north

of Bosnia, the Porte was prevailed upon to take into its consideration the disputes which had occasioned it.   Delegates
from both sides were summoned to Constantinople, and, after
long discussions, in which the officious intercession of the
Internuncio of His Majesty the Emperor and King had a share,
a Firman was obtained from the Sultan, the provisions of which
appeared at that time sufficient to conciliate successfully enough
the interests of the agricultural proprietors.   However, this
Firman has never been carried into execution.

It would not be out of place to examine, if some of the provisions of this document could not, even at the present time,
serve as the basis for an equitable arrangement suitable for the
amelioration of the condition of the rural population, or if it
would be practicable to call upon the public treasury to
facilitate the execution of the measures to be taken with this
object, in imitation of what occurred twenty years ago in
Bulgaria, where the landlord's dues have been bought up
by means of the issue of public obligations (?) called "sekims."
We feel that the task is difficult, and that its accomplishment cannot be the work of a day; but we believe that it is
important to labour at it, so as to ameliorate the lot of the rural
population in Bosnia and Herzegovina, and to close thus one
of the open wounds in the social condition of these Provinces.
It would not seem impossible to us to find some combination
which should gradually permit the peasants to acquire, on easy
terms, portions of the waste lands which the State puts up to
sell.   Whilst continuing, if they wished, to cultivate as farmers
the estates of their Mussulman compatriots, they would, by
degrees, attain to the possession themselves of a little real property, which would assure them a certain independence, and
would provide for their imposts.

If one considers the distrust with which the promises of the
Sublime Porte are received by the Christians, it is impossible to
disguise from oneself that the published reforms can only
inspire the necessary confidence by the creation at the same
time of some institution capable of offering a certain guarantee
that these reforms will be executed in earnest.   To content oneself with confiding their execution to the discretion of the
Provincial Governments would not be sufficient to remove the
distrust of which I am speaking.   It would be expedient then to
nominate a Commission of the notables of the country, composed

half of Mussulmans and half of Christians, and elected by the inhabitants of the Province in accordance with a scheme to be settled by the Sublime Porte.

I have now set forth the measures, the application of which to the revolted Provinces must be obtained to enable one to entertain a well-grounded hope of pacification.

These measures are as follows :—

Religious liberty, full and entire ;

Abolition of the farming of taxes ;

A law to guarantee that the product of the direct taxation of Bosnia and Herzegovina shall be employed for the immediate interests of the Province, under the control of bodies constituted in the sense of the Firman of December 12 ;

The institution of a Special Commission, composed of an equal number of Mussulmans and Christians, to superintend the execution of the reforms proposed by the Powers, as well as of those proclaimed in the Iradé of October 2 and Firman of December 12 ;

Lastly, the amelioration of the condition of the rural populations.

The first four points could and should be immediately carried out by the Sublime Porte ; the fifth by degrees, as soon as possible.

If, independently of these concessions, which appear to us the most essential, Bosnia and Herzegovina obtain in addition the following reforms indicated in the recent Firman, a Provincial Council and tribunals freely elected by the inhabitants, irremovability of judges, secular justice, individual liberty, security against ill-treatment, the reorganization of the police, whose conduct has excited so many complaints, the abandonment of the abuses to which the levies for public works give rise, an equitable reduction in the tax for exemption from military service, security for proprietary rights,—if all these reforms, the communication of which we claim from the Porte, in order to take formal note thereof, are applied in the insurgent Provinces, which, to judge by the text of the Firman, would not appear as yet to be in a position to benefit by them, one may hope to see peace restored in these desolated districts.

To resume. The indefinite promises of the Iradé of October 2 and Firman of December 12 can only excite aspirations without satisfying them. On the other hand, it is clear that the Turkish arms have not succeeded in putting down the insurrection. Winter has suspended action, spring will see it revive. The conviction is general among the Christians that, spring once come, fresh elements will strengthen the proceedings; that Bulgaria, the Cretans, &c. will come to swell the movement. Be this as it may, it is to be foreseen that the Governments of Servia and Montenegro, who already, up to this time, have had great difficulty in holding aloof from the movement, will be powerless to resist the current, and for the future, under the influence of events and of public opinion in their countries, they appear to have accustomed themselves to the idea of taking part in the struggle on the melting of the snows.

In this situation the task of the Powers, who in the interest of the general peace desire to stave off ulterior complications, becomes very difficult. Austria-Hungary and the two other Imperial Courts, after a confidential exchange of ideas, are all agreed that, were one merely to await the effect of the principles enunciated by the last Firman—principles which, moreover, according to the intentions of the Porte, do not appear to be intended to be immediately applied to the revolted countries— the only result would be to see the conflict widely extended at the termination of the winter. The three Cabinets then think that the only chance to avoid fresh complications is in a manifestation emanating from the Powers, and making clear their firm resolution to arrest the movement which menaces to involve the East.

Now this end cannot be attained by the simple method of an injunction addressed to the Governments of the Principalities and to the Christian populations subjects of the Sultan. To give this action, very difficult in itself, a chance of success, it is absolutely necessary that the Powers should be in a position to appeal to acts, clear, indisputable, practicable, and specially suited for the improvement of the situation of Herzegovina and Bosnia—in one word, that their action may be grounded on facts and not on programmes. It is only by these means that the Cabinets will find themselves in a position to turn to a proper account their pacific counsels.

There is another difficulty—and it is the greatest—which must, at all hazards, be overcome if one hopes to be able to reckon on any sort of a favourable result. This difficulty is the deeply-rooted distrust that every promise of the Porte's encounters at the hands of the Christians. One of the principal causes of this mistrust is discoverable in the fact that more than one measure announced in the Sultan's latest rescripts has already been announced in former Hatti-Chérifs, without causing any appreciable amelioration of the lot of the Christians.

The Cabinets think it therefore absolutely necessary to obtain from the Sultan's Government, by means of an official Commission, the confirmation of his intentions with regard to the whole Empire, set forth in the Iradé of October 2 and Firman of December 12, and his notification to the Powers of his acceptance of the points specified above, the special object of which is the pacification of the revolted Provinces.

Undoubtedly the Christians would not, by this method, obtain the form of guarantee they appear to demand at this moment, but they would find a relative security in the very fact that the reforms accorded would be recognized as indispensable by the Powers, and that the Porte would have pledged itself to Europe to carry them into execution.

Such is the firm conviction resulting from a preliminary exchange of ideas between the Cabinets of Austria, Hungary, Russia, and Germany.

Your Excellency is directed to bring this view of the case to the knowledge of the Court of St. James, and to obtain its concurrence in the work of peace, the success of which our efforts tend to assure.

If, as I hope, the views of the English Government accord with our own, we should propose, out of consideration for the dignity and independence of the Porte, not to address our advice to the latter in the form of a collective note, but to confine ourselves to inviting our Representatives at Constantinople to act conjointly and in an identic manner towards the Sultan's Government in the sense of what we have set forth.

You will be so good, M. le Comte, as to read the present despatch to the Minister for Foreign Affairs, and to leave him a copy of it, and I should be glad to know as soon as possible the impression it has made on his Excellency.

Receive, &c.

APPENDIX B.

Insurgent Camp, Sutorina, Feb. 26.

WE wish to express ourselves simply and without any disguise.
We wish to reply to certain correspondences and programmes—
to our enemies as well as to our friends ; to those who are sympathetic as well as to those who are antipathetic.

We Herzegovinians belong to a nation oppressed—a nation
enslaved for five centuries, a nation which has been, nevertheless, the source from which has sprung the noblest and purest
Serbian blood.   All Europe knows that this is the truth.

But when the sabre of the Osmans had conquered us in a
heroic combat at Kossovo, we ourselves bound our liberty with
a heavy chain.   Let us say that it was the will of God that the
glory of Mahomet should shine out, and that the cross of Jesus
should shed tears.   But we have not complained to Europe, nor
do we do so now; it was the fortune of the Turkish arms and the
effect of our discords which, as it seems, still exist among us
(in some branches of our nation), and we may, without fear or
shame, say that this discord touches our relation Servia.   It is
very painful for us to say it, although we must recognize it, that,
if there were on the throne a descendant of the immortal Kara
George, or a direct descendant of Milosch, he could not hear the
cries of our martyrs without being touched.

In truth, the noble spirit of the dead Prince Milosch—if we
were as happy to have it as we are unhappy with not having it—
would not have counted by feet the depth of the sea nor the
height of the heaven in a critical moment.   He would not have

looked about him to the right and to the left, but would have taken the direct road to poor Bosnia and Herzegovina. But, alas! . . . .

On the other side we hear, but understand nothing of all these projects of reform that some European Cabinets have formed, in order that the oppressed Christians of Turkey should obtain equality with Mussulmans. For it is not only uncertain, but impracticable. In these projects of reform there is not a word said as to real liberty—liberty, independent and securely guaranteed by the Powers of Europe.

That is the project of reform we need.

Such reforms suit us; if not, give us the tomb which will bury us, and where we may go down, quitting the world.

The friends of our country, whether they are such or seem as much so as possible, think that they have a reason or a right to hear and support the barbarous savages from Asia who have conquered us, have caused our discords, and who, among the other nations, are only as leprous sheep in a healthy flock.

We repeat—only true liberty can disarm us, and to crush us there is need of more numerous arms than those of the Osmans; and then the women will remain after us to avenge us, receiving from our hands arms for our children that they may, even in dying, defend the liberty and rights of our people. All the more that the hand of the stranger is on us, we beg the friends and defenders of our country to aid and to avenge us.

Aid us! hear us! now or never! . . . .

Austria, in its position of neighbouring State, did and still does good to our children, our old men and our women. Eternal gratitude to her from our chiefs and from our nation!

The immortal Liberator, Italy's crown of glory, Garibaldi, assists us energetically, and shows himself the protecting father of our oppressed people. Blessed be he by us and our descendants.

Powerful England, the greatest friend of the Turkish Empire, held it in her arms believing that she held a worthy child, which would grow into a honest man, magnanimous and useful to other nations. But she has opened her eyes and perceives that, instead of a man, she has supported a venomous serpent, which, grown great and strong, and for the sorrow of humanity, endeavoured to poison and devour it, and at last even would have bitten the hand that had given it to eat. This powerful kingdom has

launched it into the deadly abyss, and, hearing our cries, has
given us its support, for which we owe it eternal gratitude.

Our brothers, our true brothers, the noble Serbian blood, the
proud sons of the Voivodina, watch day and night over and for
our liberty, as the mother and father over the cradle of their only
son or daughter, ill.   To the noble line of this race, in the midst
of whom we see and hear the name of Miletich, we can say
nothing, but we counsel our descendants to honour it.

That which, however, we regret is that they do not endeavour
to inform our brothers in Servia that we are now in full combat
with the Turks, that our old men and women are falling victims
to a thousand woes, and that our country prays for their brotherly
aid, and that our blood while it flows demands vengeance of our
sister Servia.   In truth, if they heard us they would help us, but
they are so far (not by measurement of earth) from us ! . . . .
Therefore we beg our brothers of the Voivodina to spread the
news everywhere and repeat to every one that the houses of
Montenegro are filled with our refugees, and that their number
has become greater than that of the population was, yet that they
nevertheless do not complain ; on the contrary, their fraternal
arms are always open.   Nevertheless, we demand of Montenegro
as of Servia that it should enter openly into the field, and that it
should find out our spilt blood, which cries out for vengeance,
not looking towards Servia, apathetic and neutral, so far from us.

The combinations of diplomacy over which the world may de-
bate and agree are not our affair.   Our true and holy object is
to-day to confront the enemy for our defence, and to watch on
every side lest fortune, which has hitherto protected us, should
betray us.   We go on to fight, to burn, and to conquer.

We can only become tranquil under the happiness of the
liberty of which Montenegro shows us the example.

We look unitedly, we hope and wait that the powerful, strong,
and glorious Russia should appear as the protector of Slavo-Serb
liberty—now or never !   If she has ever loved or desired our
liberty, may our morning receive its light from the powerful
goodwill of her illustrious throne.   It is from her that we hope
for the protection of our liberty, but we ask of the other European
nations that they give us our independence.   And our arms, once
freed from all encumbrances, will write in bloody letters for the
Turks the reforms they have so often dictated to us.

As to Prussia, glorious and free, we do not doubt that she is

our friend, and we hope to find her among those who the first
will aid our liberty, for which we ask her pity.

Signed for the Army and the Chiefs of the Insurgents at
Sutorina,

> VOIVODE LAZAR SOCICA.
> MELENTIE PEROVICS, Archimandrite.
> VOIVODE POPE BOGDAN (SIMONICS).

Then appears, as a protocol, the following :—

Anew we call on the Power of Russia, which has conferred on
us benefits in offering us money to build our churches and our
schools ; which has given us crosses and gilded robes for the
Mass, &c. But while our poor priests celebrated the Mass in
those same robes, the Mussulmans dishonoured their women in
their houses. Because Russia cannot be deaf and cruel, she will
watch over our holy rites and our independence in order that we
may not rest eternally slaves. We desire only complete independence, or death. We sign with our blood this declaration,
and accept no other proposition.

(Signed as before.)

APPENDIX C.

EXCELLENCY,—

NONE can more appreciate the rectitude, nor recognize with more sincere gratitude the undertaking of powerful Austria in thus attempting to ameliorate the condition of the Christians in Turkey, and of us insurgents—a condition so wretched as to have become henceforth insupportable.

The Imperial Austrian Government may be assured that the Herzegovinian nation is profoundly touched, and grateful for all that that Government has done for our good. We, having been obedient to the summons of Austria, and desirous of following her counsels, ask permission of your Excellency, as of a friendly intermediary with the Imperial Government, to say frankly what we have at heart, and what we desire, especially as we think and believe that no one in the world can expect that we shall return into the power of the Turks, and into the condition in which we have lived hitherto ; as also that no one in the world can desire that we should so return.

Everything in our country is burned and laid waste. With what spirit can we return to this unhappy country of ours?

Austria has been so good as to interest herself about us and our existence, and has informed us that she has obtained some reform for us. In the words of Austria we have trust, and therefore we accept these reforms, but only when they shall have been put into execution, then will we return under the sovereignty of the Sultan.

It is true Turkey has promised to execute them, and says that the Powers have guaranteed them, but we cannot on any account believe that Turkey means to or can execute them. Therefore, no sincere friend of our unhappy nation will think we are wrong in seeking for secure guarantees for our amelioration, which guarantees we submit and present to your Excellency :—

I. That to the Christians shall be given at least a third of the lands as their property—lands which the Turks took and usurped from the Christians, and without which third the latter will not be able to live.[1]

II. That Turkey withdraws the troops in the Herzegovina and shall only maintain garrisons which shall be recognized as necessary in the following places : Mostar, Stolatz, Trebinje, Niksics, Plevljé, and Fotcha.

III. That Turkey cause to be rebuilt the houses and churches that have been burned, provide for the Christians food for at least a year, and agricultural implements, and exempt them from taxation for three years from the date of their return.

IV. That the Christians shall not lay down their arms until the Mussulmans shall have been disarmed, and until the reforms are in process of execution.

V. The Christians having returned, their leaders shall come to an understanding with the Government as to the execution of the reforms. The said leaders shall compose an assembly with the functionaries of the Government for the application and the regulation of the said reforms, which latter must be extended to the whole of Bosnia and the Herzegovina.

VI. As the insurgents cannot trust to the simple promises of the Porte, which it has never been known to keep, and as also the Porte will with difficulty support its own troops, the insur-

---

[1] Since writing the above, I have seen the report which M. Durando sends this day to his Government upon the Address of the insurgents. He points out that the demand for a third of the lands must not be considered as indicative of communistic aspirations, but as a clumsily expressed desire for the revocation of the agrarian regulations of 1851 and 1862, which abolished the ancient feudal privileges of the tillers of the soil.—Mr. MONSON (Blue Book).

The original tenure of land in Bosnia, &c., was communal, the Beys having only a feudal right of contribution in return for personal protection. The assumption of exclusive property in the land was a usurpation favoured by Islam.—W. J. S.

gents fearing that the money given by the Porte for the Christians may be lost in the hands of the Turkish employés, who would distribute nothing, and would let the Christians starve ; and as the insurgents know that they would get no help from the Porte, even if the Powers should protest :—on these grounds, we demand that the money shall be paid into the hands of the Treasurer of a European Commission ; that this Commission shall receive all the funds for the reconstruction by itself of the houses and churches, and for the distribution of provisions to the Christian families, erecting for that purpose central store-houses in convenient places.

Finally, we demand that in the before-mentioned garrisons, occupied by the Turks, the Governments of Austria and Russia shall establish agents, who shall see that the reforms are executed as we desire.

While we do not dare to ask for more, we cannot, on the other hand, ask for less for our safety and tranquillity.   -

We submit these our desires to Austria through the medium of your Excellency.

Sutorina, March 26 / April 7, 1876.

APPENDIX D.

THE alarming tidings which come from Turkey are of a nature to impel the three Cabinets to draw closer their intimacy.

The three Imperial Courts have deemed themselves called upon to concert amongst themselves measures for averting the dangers of the situation, with the concurrence of the other great Christian Powers.

It appears to them that the existing state of affairs in Turkey demands a double series of measures. It seems to them of primary importance that Europe should consider the general means necessary to guard against the recurrence of events similar to those which have recently taken place at Salonica, and the repetition of which is threatened at Smyrna and Constantinople. To effect this the Great Powers should, in their opinion, come to an understanding as to the measures to be taken to insure the safety of their own subjects and of the Christian inhabitants of the Ottoman Empire, at all points where it may be found to be endangered.

It would appear possible to attain this end by a general agreement concerning the despatch of vessels of war to the menaced points, and by the adoption of combined instructions to the commanders of those vessels in cases where circumstances might require armed co-operation on their part with the object of maintaining order and tranquillity.

Nevertheless, this end would be but imperfectly attained if the primary cause of those disturbances were not removed by the prompt pacification of Bosnia and Herzegovina.

The Great Powers have already united in this view upon the initiative taken in the despatch of the 30th of December last, with the object of obtaining an effective amelioration in the condition of the populations of these countries, without interfering with the political *status quo.*

They demanded of the Porte a programme of reforms destined to answer this double purpose. The Porte, deferring to this demand, declared itself firmly resolved to execute these reforms, and communicated this officially to the Cabinets.

The latter thereby acquire a moral right—that of watching over the accomplishment of this promise, and an obligation—that of insisting that the insurgents and refugees should second this work of pacification by terminating the struggle and returning to their homes.

Nevertheless, this programme of pacification, though it has been adopted in principle by both parties, has encountered a twofold obstacle.

The insurgents have declared that past experience forbids them to trust the promises of the Porte, without a positive material European guarantee.

The Porte, on its side, has declared that, as long as the insurgents were scouring the country in arms, and the refugees did not return to their homes, it was materially impossible for it to proceed to the new organization of the country.

In the meantime hostilities have resumed their course. The agitation engendered by this strife of eight months has extended to other parts of Turkey. The Mussulman populations have been thereby led to conclude that the Porte had only apparently deferred to the diplomatic action of Europe, and that at heart it did not intend seriously to apply the promised reforms. Thence arose a revival of religious and political passions, which has contributed to cause the deplorable events at Salonica and the menacing over-excitement which manifests itself at other points of European Turkey.

Nor is it doubtful that in its turn this explosion of fanaticism reacts on men's minds in Bosnia and Herzegovina as in the neighbouring Principalities.

For the Christians in these countries must have been keenly impressed by the fact of the massacre of the European Consuls, in open day, in a peaceful town, under the eyes of powerless authorities ; how can they be induced to trust themselves to the goodwill of Turks irritated by a protracted and sanguinary struggle?

Were this state of affairs to be prolonged the risk would thus be incurred of seeing that general conflagration kindled which the mediation of the Great Powers was precisely intended to avert.

It is most essential, therefore, to establish certain guarantees of a nature to insure beyond doubt the loyal and full application of the measures agreed upon between the Powers and the Porte. It is more than ever urgent to press the Government of the Sultan to decide on setting itself seriously to work to fulfil the engagements it has contracted towards Europe.

As the first step in this direction the three Imperial Courts propose to insist with the Porte, with all the energy that the united voice of the three Powers should possess, on a suspension of arms being effected for the term of two months.

This interval would enable action to be brought to bear simultaneously on the insurgents and the refugees, to inspire them with confidence in the vigilant solicitude of Europe ; on the neighbouring Principalities, to exhort them not to hinder this attempt at conciliation ; and finally on the Ottoman Government, to place it in a position to carry out its promises. By this means the way might be opened for direct negotiations between the Porte and the Bosnian and Herzegovinian delegates, on the basis of the wishes the latter have formulated, and which have been deemed fit to serve as starting points for a discussion.

These points are as follows :—

1. That materials for the reconstruction of dwelling-houses and churches should be furnished to the returning refugees, that their subsistence should be assured to them till they could support themselves by their own labour.

2. In so far as the distribution of help should appertain to the Turkish Commissioner, he should consult as to the measures to be taken with the Mixed Commission, mentioned in the note of the 30th of December, to guarantee the *bonâ fide* application of the reforms and control their execution. This Commission should be presided over by a Herzegovinian Christian, and be composed of natives faithfully representing the two religions of the country. They should be elected as soon as the armistice should have suspended hostilities.

3. In order to avoid any collision, advice should be given at Constantinople to concentrate the Turkish troops, at least until excitement has subsided, on some points to be agreed upon.

4. Christians as well as Mussulmans should retain their arms.

5. The Consuls or Delegates of the Powers should keep a watch over the application of the reforms in general, and on the steps relative to the repatriation in particular.

If, with the friendly and cordial support of the great Powers, and by the help of an armistice, an arrangement could be concluded on these bases, and be set in train immediately by the return of the refugees, and the election of the Mixed Commission, a considerable step would be made towards pacification.

If, however, the armistice were to expire without the efforts of the Powers being successful in attaining the end they have in view, the three Imperial Courts are of opinion that it would become necessary to supplement their diplomatic action by the sanction of an agreement with a view to such efficacious measures as might appear to be demanded in the interest of general peace, to check the evil and prevent its development.

INDEX.

CHISWICK PRESS:—C. WHITTINGHAM, TOOKS COURT,
CHANCERY LANE.

GENERAL LIST OF WORKS

PUBLISHED BY

Messrs. LONGMANS, GREEN, and CO.

PATERNOSTER ROW, LONDON.

——∘⚬⦂⊗⦂⚬∘——

History, Politics, Historical Memoirs, &c.

The HISTORY of ENGLAND from the Accession of James the Second.
By Lord MACAULAY.

> STUDENT'S EDITION, 2 vols. crown 8vo. 12s.
> PEOPLE'S EDITION, 4 vols. crown 8vo. 16s.
> CABINET EDITION, 8 vols. post 8vo. 48s.
> LIBRARY EDITION, 5 vols. 8vo. £4.

LORD MACAULAY'S WORKS. Complete and Uniform Library Edition. Edited by his Sister, Lady TREVELYAN. 8 vols. 8vo. with Portrait price £5. 5s. cloth, or £8. 8s. bound in tree-calf by Rivière.

The HISTORY of ENGLAND from the Fall of Wolsey to the Defeat of the Spanish Armada. By JAMES ANTHONY FROUDE, M.A. late Fellow of Exeter College, Oxford.

> LIBRARY EDITION, Twelve Volumes, 8vo. price £8. 18s.
> CABINET EDITION, Twelve Volumes, crown 8vo. price 72s.

The ENGLISH in IRELAND in the EIGHTEENTH CENTURY. By JAMES ANTHONY FROUDE, M.A. late Fellow of Exeter College, Oxford. 3 vols. 8vo. price 48s.

JOURNAL of the REIGNS of KING GEORGE IV. and KING WILLIAM IV. By the late CHARLES C. F. GREVILLE, Esq. Edited by HENRY REEVE, Esq. Fifth Edition. 3 vols. 8vo. 36s.

RECOLLECTIONS and SUGGESTIONS, 1813–1873. By JOHN Earl RUSSELL, K.G. New Edition, revised and enlarged. 8vo. 16s.

On PARLIAMENTARY GOVERNMENT in ENGLAND; its Origin, Development, and Practical Operation. By ALPHEUS TODD, Librarian of the Legislative Assembly of Canada. 2 vols. 8vo. price £1. 17s.

The CONSTITUTIONAL HISTORY of ENGLAND, since the Accession of George III. 1760–1860. By Sir THOMAS ERSKINE MAY, K.C.B. D.C.L. The Fifth Edition, thoroughly revised. 3 vols. crown 8vo. price 18s.

DEMOCRACY in EUROPE; a History. By Sir THOMAS ERSKINE MAY, K.C.B. D.C.L. 2 vols. 8vo.   [*In the press.*

The NEW REFORMATION, a Narrative of the Old Catholic Movement, from 1870 to the Present Time; with an Historical Introduction. By THEODORUS. 8vo. price 12s.

A

The OXFORD REFORMERS — John Colet, Erasmus, and Thomas
More ; being a History of their Fellow-work. By FREDERIC SEEBOHM.
Second Edition, enlarged. 8vo. 14s.

LECTURES on the HISTORY of ENGLAND, from the Earliest Times
to the Death of King Edward II. By WILLIAM LONGMAN, F.S.A. With Maps
and Illustrations. 8vo. 15s.

The HISTORY of the LIFE and TIMES of EDWARD the THIRD.
By WILLIAM LONGMAN, F.S.A. With 9 Maps, 8 Plates, and 16 Woodcuts.
2 vols. 8vo. 28s.

INTRODUCTORY LECTURES on MODERN HISTORY. Delivered
in Lent Term, 1842; with the Inaugural Lecture delivered in December 1841.
By the Rev. THOMAS ARNOLD, D.D. 8vo. price 7s. 6d.

WATERLOO LECTURES ; a Study of the Campaign of 1815. By
Colonel CHARLES C. CHESNEY, R.E. Third Edition. 8vo. with Map, 10s. 6d.

HISTORY of ENGLAND under the DUKE of BUCKINGHAM and
CHARLES the FIRST, 1624–1628. By SAMUEL RAWSON GARDINER, late
Student of Ch. Ch. 2 vols. 8vo. with two Maps, price 24s.

The SIXTH ORIENTAL MONARCHY ; or, the Geography, History,
and Antiquities of PARTHIA. By GEORGE RAWLINSON, M.A. Professor of
Ancient History in the University of Oxford. Maps and Illustrations. 8vo. 16s.

The SEVENTH GREAT ORIENTAL MONARCHY ; or, a History of
the SASSANIANS: with Notices, Geographical and Antiquarian. By G.
RAWLINSON, M.A. Map and numerous Illustrations. 8vo. price 28s.

A HISTORY of GREECE. By the Rev. GEORGE W. COX, M.A. late
Scholar of Trinity College, Oxford. VOLS. I. & II. (to the Close of the Peloponnesian War). 8vo. with Maps and Plans, 36s.

GENERAL HISTORY of GREECE to the Death of Alexander the
Great ; with a Sketch of the Subsequent History to the Present Time. By the
Rev. GEORGE W. Cox, M.A. With 11 Maps. Crown 8vo. 7s. 6d.

The GREEKS and the PERSIANS. By the Rev. GEORGE W. Cox,
M.A. (Epochs of Ancient History, I.) With 4 Coloured Maps. Fcp. 8vo.
price 2s. 6d.

The TALE of the GREAT PERSIAN WAR, from the Histories of
Herodotus. By GEORGE W. COX, M.A. New Edition. Fcp. 3s. 6d.

The HISTORY of ROME. By WILLIAM IHNE. VOLS. I. and II.
8vo. price 30s. The Third Volume is in the press.

GENERAL HISTORY OF ROME from the Foundation of the City to
the Fall of Augustulus, B.C. 753—A.D. 476. By the Very Rev. C. MERIVALE,
D.D. Dean of Ely. With Five Maps. Crown 8vo. 7s. 6d.

HISTORY of the ROMANS under the EMPIRE. By the Very Rev.
C. MERIVALE, D.D. Dean of Ely. 8 vols. post 8vo. 48s.

The FALL of the ROMAN REPUBLIC ; a Short History of the Last
Century of the Commonwealth. By the same Author. 12mo. 7s. 6d.

The STUDENT'S MANUAL of the HISTORY of INDIA, from the
Earliest Period to the Present. By Colonel MEADOWS TAYLOR, M.R.A.S.
M.R.I.A. Second Thousand. Crown 8vo. with Maps, 7s. 6d.

The HISTORY of INDIA, from the Earliest Period to the close of Lord
Dalhousie's Administration. By J. C. MARSHMAN. 3 vols. crown 8vo. 22s. 6d.

The **NATIVE STATES of INDIA in SUBSIDIARY ALLIANCE** with the BRITISH GOVERNMENT; an Historical Sketch. By Colonel G. B. MALLESON, C.S.I. With 6 Coloured Maps. 8vo. 15s.

INDIAN POLITY; a View of the System of Administration in India. By Lieutenant-Colonel GEORGE CHESNEY, Fellow of the University of Calcutta. New Edition, revised; with Map. 8vo. price 21s.

The **BRITISH ARMY in 1875**; with Suggestions on its Administration and Organisation. By JOHN HOLMS, M.P. New and Enlarged Edition, with 4 Diagrams. Crown 8vo. price 4s. 6d.

The **HISTORY of PRUSSIA**, from the Earliest Times to the Present Day; tracing the Origin and Development of her Military Organisation. By Captain W. J. WYATT. Vols. I. and II. A.D. 700 to A.D. 1525. 8vo. 36s.

POPULAR HISTORY of FRANCE, from the Earliest Times to the Death of Louis XIV. By ELIZABETH M. SEWELL, Author of ' Amy Herbert' &c. With Coloured Maps. Crown 8vo. 7s. 6d.

STUDIES from GENOESE HISTORY. By Colonel G. B. MALLESON, C.S.I. Guardian to His Highness the Maharája of Mysore. Crown 8vo. 10s. 6d.

LORD MACAULAY'S CRITICAL and HISTORICAL ESSAYS. CHEAP EDITION, authorised and complete. Crown 8vo. 3s. 6d.

CABINET EDITION, 4 vols. post 8vo. 24s.	LIBRARY EDITION, 3 vols. 8vo. 36s.
PEOPLE'S EDITION, 2 vols. crown 8vo. 8s.	STUDENT'S EDITION, 1 vol. cr. 8vo. 6s.

HISTORY of EUROPEAN MORALS, from Augustus to Charlemagne. By W. E. H. LECKY, M.A. Second Edition. 2 vols. 8vo. price 28s.

HISTORY of the RISE and INFLUENCE of the SPIRIT of RATIONALISM in EUROPE. By W. E. H. LECKY, M.A. Cabinet Edition, being the Fourth. 2 vols. crown 8vo. price 16s.

The **HISTORY of PHILOSOPHY, from Thales to Comte.** By GEORGE HENRY LEWES. Fourth Edition. 2 vols. 8vo. 32s.

The **HISTORY of the PELOPONNESIAN WAR.** By THUCYDIDES. Translated by R. CRAWLEY, Fellow of Worcester College, Oxford. 8vo. 10s. 6d.

The **MYTHOLOGY of the ARYAN NATIONS.** By GEORGE W. COX, M.A. late Scholar of Trinity College, Oxford. 2 vols. 8vo. 28s.

TALES of ANCIENT GREECE. By GEORGE W. COX, M.A. late Scholar of Trin. Coll. Oxon. Crown 8vo. price 6s. 6d.

HISTORY of CIVILISATION in England and France, Spain and Scotland. By HENRY THOMAS BUCKLE. New Edition of the entire Work, with a complete INDEX. 3 vols. crown 8vo. 24s.

SKETCH of the HISTORY of the CHURCH of ENGLAND to the Revolution of 1688. By the Right Rev. T. V. SHORT, D.D. Lord Bishop of St. Asaph. Eighth Edition. Crown 8vo. 7s. 6d.

MAUNDER'S HISTORICAL TREASURY; General Introductory Outlines of Universal History, and a series of Separate Histories. Latest Edition, revised by the Rev. G. W. COX, M.A. Fcp. 8vo. 6s. cloth, or 10s. 6d. calf.

CATES' and WOODWARD'S ENCYCLOPÆDIA of CHRONOLOGY, HISTORICAL and BIOGRAPHICAL. 8vo. price 42s.

The **ERA of the PROTESTANT REVOLUTION.** By F. SEEBOHM. With 4 Coloured Maps and 12 Diagrams on Wood. Fcp. 8vo. 2s. 6d.

The CRUSADES. By the Rev. G. W. Cox, M.A. late Scholar of Trinity
College, Oxford. With Coloured Map. Fcp. 8vo. 2s. 6d.

The THIRTY YEARS' WAR, 1618-1648. By SAMUEL RAWSON GAR-
DINER, late Student of Christ Church. With Coloured Map. Fcp. 8vo. 2s. 6d.

The HOUSES of LANCASTER and YORK; with the Conquest and
Loss of France. By JAMES GAIRDNER, of the Public Record Office. With Five
Coloured Maps. Fcp. 8vo. 2s. 6d.

EDWARD the THIRD. By the Rev. W. WARBURTON, M.A. late
Fellow of All Souls College, Oxford. With 3 Coloured Maps and 8 Genealogical
Tables. Fcp. 8vo. 2s. 6d.

The AGE of ELIZABETH. By the Rev. M. CREIGHTON, M.A. late
Fellow and Tutor of Merton College, Oxford. With 5 Maps and 4 Genealogical
Tables. Fcp. 8vo. 2s. 6d.

The FALL of the STUARTS; and Western Europe from 1678 to
1697. By the Rev. E. HALE, M.A. Assistant-Master, Eton. With 11 Maps and
Plans. Fcp. 8vo. 2s. 6d.

The FIRST TWO STUARTS and the PURITAN REVOLUTION,
1603-1660. By SAMUEL RAWSON GARDINER, late Student of Christ Church.
With 4 Coloured Maps. Fcp. 8vo. 2s. 6d.

The WAR of AMERICAN INDEPENDENCE, 1775-1783. By
JOHN MALCOLM LUDLOW, Barrister-at-Law. With 4 Coloured Maps. Fcp.
8vo. 2s. 6d.

REALITIES of IRISH LIFE. By W. STEUART TRENCH, late Land
Agent in Ireland to the Marquess of Lansdowne, the Marquess of Bath, and
Lord Digby. Cheaper Edition. Crown 8vo. price 2s. 6d.

Biographical Works.

The LIFE and LETTERS of LORD MACAULAY. By his Nephew,
G. OTTO TREVELYAN, M.P. 2 vols. 8vo. with Portrait, price 36s.

The LIFE of SIR WILLIAM FAIRBAIRN, Bart. F.R.S. Corresponding Member of the National Institute of France, &c. Partly written by
himself; edited and completed by WILLIAM POLE, F.R.S.   [In the Press.

ARTHUR SCHOPENHAUER, his LIFE and his PHILOSOPHY.
By HELEN ZIMMERN. Post 8vo. with Portrait, 7s. 6d.

MEMOIRS of BARON STOCKMAR. By his Son, Baron E. VON
STOCKMAR. Translated from the German by G. A. M. Edited by F. MAX
MÜLLER, M.A. 2 vols. crown 8vo. 21s.

AUTOBIOGRAPHY. By JOHN STUART MILL. 8vo. price 7s. 6d.

The LIFE of NAPOLEON III. derived from State Records, Unpublished
Family Correspondence, and Personal Testimony. By BLANCHARD JERROLD.
4 vols. 8vo. with numerous Portraits and Facsimiles. VOLS. I. and II. price 18s.
each. The Third Volume is in the press.

LIFE and LETTERS of Sir GILBERT ELLIOT, First EARL of
MINTO. Edited by the COUNTESS of MINTO. 3 vols. 8vo. 31s. 6d.

ESSAYS in MODERN MILITARY BIOGRAPHY. By CHARLES
CORNWALLIS CHESNEY, Lieutenant-Colonel in the Royal Engineers. 8vo. 12s. 6d.

The MEMOIRS of SIR JOHN RERESBY, of Thrybergh, Bart. M.P.
for York, &c. 1634—1689. Written by Himself. Edited from the Original
Manuscript by JAMES J. CARTWRIGHT, M.A. 8vo. price 21s.

ISAAC CASAUBON, 1559-1614. By MARK PATTISON, Rector of Lincoln College, Oxford. 8vo. 18s.

LORD GEORGE BENTINCK; a Political Biography. By the Right Hon. BENJAMIN DISRAELI, M.P. Crown 8vo. price 6s.

LEADERS of PUBLIC OPINION in **IRELAND**; Swift, Flood, Grattan, and O'Connell. By W. E. H. LECKY, M.A. New Edition, revised and enlarged. Crown 8vo. price 7s. 6d.

DICTIONARY of GENERAL BIOGRAPHY; containing Concise Memoirs and Notices of the most Eminent Persons of all Countries, from the Earliest Ages. By W. L. R. CATES. New Edition, extended in a Supplement to the Year 1875. Medium 8vo. price 25s.

LIFE of the DUKE of WELLINGTON. By the Rev. G. R. GLEIG, M.A. Popular Edition, carefully revised ; with copious Additions. Crown 8vo. with Portrait, 5s.

MEMOIRS of SIR HENRY HAVELOCK, K.C.B. By JOHN CLARK MARSHMAN. Cabinet Edition, with Portrait. Crown 8vo. price 3s. 6d.

VICISSITUDES of FAMILIES. By Sir J. BERNARD BURKE, C.B. Ulster King of Arms. New Edition, enlarged. 2 vols. crown 8vo. 21s.

The RISE of GREAT FAMILIES, other Essays and Stories. By Sir J. BERNARD BURKE, C.B. Ulster King of Arms. Crown 8vo. price 12s. 6d.

ESSAYS in ECCLESIASTICAL BIOGRAPHY. By the Right Hon. Sir J. STEPHEN, LL.D. Cabinet Edition. Crown 8vo. 7s. 6d.

MAUNDER'S BIOGRAPHICAL TREASURY. Latest Edition, reconstructed, thoroughly revised, and in great part rewritten ; with 1,000 additional Memoirs and Notices, by W. L. R. CATES. Fcp. 8vo. 6s. cloth ; 10s. 6d. calf.

LETTERS and LIFE of FRANCIS BACON, including all his Occasional Works. Collected and edited, with a Commentary, by J. SPEDDING, Trin. Coll. Cantab. Complete in 7 vols. 8vo. £4. 4s.

The LIFE, WORKS, and OPINIONS of HEINRICH HEINE. By WILLIAM STIGAND. 2 vols. 8vo. with Portrait of Heine, price 28s.

BIOGRAPHICAL and CRITICAL ESSAYS, reprinted from Reviews, with Additions and Corrections. Second Edition of the Second Series. By A. HAYWARD, Q.C. 2 vols. 8vo. price 28s. THIRD SERIES, in 1 vol. 8vo. price 14s.

Criticism, Philosophy, Polity, &c.

The LAW of NATIONS considered as INDEPENDENT POLITICAL COMMUNITIES ; the Rights and Duties of Nations in Time of War. By Sir TRAVERS TWISS, D.C.L., F.R.S. New Edition, revised ; with an Introductory Juridical Review of the Results of Recent Wars, and an Appendix of Treaties and other Documents. 8vo. 21s.

CHURCH and STATE: their relations Historically Developed. By T. HEINRICH GEFFCKEN, Professor of International Law at the University of Strasburg. Translated from the German by E. FAIRFAX TAYLOR. [In the press.

A SYSTEMATIC VIEW of the SCIENCE of JURISPRUDENCE. By SHELDON AMOS, M.A. Professor of Jurisprudence to the Inns of Court, London. 8vo. price 18s.

A PRIMER of the ENGLISH CONSTITUTION and GOVERNMENT.
By SHELDON AMOS, M.A. Professor of Jurisprudence to the Inns of Court.
Second Edition, revised. Crown 8vo. 6s.

OUTLINES of CIVIL PROCEDURE. Being a General View of the
Supreme Court of Judicature and of the whole Practice in the Common Law and
Chancery Divisions under all the Statutes now in force. By EDWARD STANLEY
ROSCOE, Barrister-at-Law. 12mo. price 3s. 6d.

The INSTITUTES of JUSTINIAN; with English Introduction, Translation and Notes. By T. C. SANDARS, M.A. Sixth Edition. 8vo. 18s.

SOCRATES and the SOCRATIC SCHOOLS. Translated from the
German of Dr. E. ZELLER, with the Author's approval, by the Rev. OSWALD J.
REICHEL, M.A. Crown 8vo. 8s. 6d.

The STOICS, EPICUREANS, and SCEPTICS. Translated from the
German of Dr. E. ZELLER, with the Author's approval, by OSWALD J. REICHEL,
M.A. Crown 8vo. price 14s.

PLATO and the OLDER ACADEMY. Translated from the German
of Dr. EDUARD ZELLER by S. FRANCES ALLEYNE and ALFRED GOODWIN, B.A.
Fellow of Balliol College, Oxford. Crown 8vo. 18s.

The ETHICS of ARISTOTLE, with Essays and Notes. By Sir A.
GRANT, Bart. M.A. LL.D. Third Edition. 2 vols. 8vo. 32s.

The POLITICS of ARISTOTLE; Greek Text, with English Notes. By
RICHARD CONGREVE, M.A. New Edition, revised. 8vo. 18s.

The NICOMACHEAN ETHICS of ARISTOTLE newly translated into
English. By R. WILLIAMS, B.A. Fellow and late Lecturer of Merton College,
and sometime Student of Christ Church, Oxford. New Edition. 8vo. 7s. 6d.

PICTURE LOGIC; an Attempt to Popularise the Science of Reasoning by the combination of Humorous Pictures with Examples of Reasoning
taken from Daily Life. By A. SWINBOURNE, B.A. With Woodcut Illustrations from Drawings by the Author. Second Edition. Fcp. 8vo. price 5s.

ELEMENTS of LOGIC. By R. WHATELY, D.D. late Archbishop of
Dublin. New Edition. 8vo. 10s. 6d. crown 8vo. 4s. 6d.

Elements of Rhetoric. By the same Author. New Edition. 8vo.
10s. 6d. crown 8vo. 4s. 6d.

English Synonymes. By E. JANE WHATELY. Edited by Archbishop
WHATELY. Fifth Edition. Fcp. 8vo. price 3s.

On the INFLUENCE of AUTHORITY in MATTERS of OPINION.
By the late Sir GEORGE CORNEWALL LEWIS, Bart. New Edition. 8vo. 14s.

COMTE'S SYSTEM of POSITIVE POLITY, or TREATISE upon
SOCIOLOGY. Translated from the Paris Edition of 1851-1854, and furnished
with Analytical Tables of Contents. In Four Volumes, 8vo. each forming in
some degree an independent Treatise :—

VOL. I. General View of Positivism and its Introductory Principles. Translated
by J. H. BRIDGES, M.B. Price 21s.

VOL. II. Social Statics, or the Abstract Laws of Human Order. Translated by
F. HARRISON, M.A. Price 14s.

VOL. III. Social Dynamics, or the General Laws of Human Progress (the
Philosophy of History). Translated by Professor E. S. BEESLY, M.A. 8vo. 21s.

VOL. IV. Synthesis of the Future of Mankind. Translated by R. CONGREVE,
M.D.; and an Appendix, containing the Author's Minor Treatises, translated by
H. D. Hutton, M.A.   [In the press.

DEMOCRACY in AMERICA. By ALEXIS DE TOCQUEVILLE. Translated by HENRY REEVE, Esq. New Edition. 2 vols. crown 8vo. 16s.

ORDER and PROGRESS: Part I. Thoughts on Government; Part II. Studies of Political Crises. By FREDERIC HARRISON, M.A. of Lincoln's Inn. 8vo. price 14s.

BACON'S ESSAYS with ANNOTATIONS. By R. WHATELY, D.D. late Archbishop of Dublin. New Edition, 8vo. price 10s. 6d.

LORD BACON'S WORKS, collected and edited by J. SPEDDING, M.A. R. L. ELLIS, M.A. and D. D. HEATH. 7 vols. 8vo. price £3. 13s. 6d.

On REPRESENTATIVE GOVERNMENT. By JOHN STUART MILL Crown 8vo. price 2s.

On LIBERTY. By JOHN STUART MILL. New Edition. Post 8vo. 7s. 6d. Crown 8vo. price 1s. 4d.

PRINCIPLES of POLITICAL ECONOMY. By JOHN STUART MILL. Seventh Edition. 2 vols. 8vo. 30s. Or in 1 vol. crown 8vo. price 5s.

ESSAYS on SOME UNSETTLED QUESTIONS of POLITICAL ECONOMY. By JOHN STUART MILL. Second Edition. 8vo. 6s. 6d.

UTILITARIANISM. By JOHN STUART MILL. New Edition. 8vo. 5s.

DISSERTATIONS and DISCUSSIONS: Political, Philosophical, and Historical. By JOHN STUART MILL. New Editions. 4 vols. 8vo. price £2. 6s. 6d.

EXAMINATION of Sir. W. HAMILTON'S PHILOSOPHY, and of the Principal Philosophical Questions discussed in his Writings. By JOHN STUART MILL. Fourth Edition. 8vo. 16s.

An OUTLINE of the NECESSARY LAWS of THOUGHT; a Treatise on Pure and Applied Logic. By the Most Rev. W. THOMSON, Lord Archbishop of York, D.D. F.R.S. New Edition. Crown 8vo. price 6s.

PRINCIPLES of ECONOMICAL PHILOSOPHY. By HENRY DUNNING MACLEOD, M.A. Barrister-at-Law. Second Edition. In Two Volumes. VOL. I. 8vo. price 15s. VOL. II. PART I. price 12s. VOL. II. PART II. just ready.

A SYSTEM of LOGIC, RATIOCINATIVE and INDUCTIVE. By JOHN STUART MILL. Ninth Edition. Two vols. 8vo. 25s.

SPEECHES of the RIGHT HON. LORD MACAULAY, corrected by Himself. People's Edition, crown 8vo. 3s. 6d.

The ORATION of DEMOSTHENES on the CROWN. Translated by the Right Hon. Sir R. P. COLLIER. Crown 8vo. price 5s.

FAMILIES of SPEECH: Four Lectures delivered before the Royal Institution of Great Britain. By the Rev. F. W. FARRAR, D.D. F.R.S. New Edition. Crown 8vo. 3s. 6d.

CHAPTERS on LANGUAGE. By the Rev. F. W. FARRAR, D.D. F.R.S. New Edition. Crown 8vo. 5s.

HANDBOOK of the ENGLISH LANGUAGE. For the use of Students of the Universities and the Higher Classes in Schools. By R. G. LATHAM, M.A. M.D. The Ninth Edition. Crown 8vo. price 6s.

DICTIONARY of the ENGLISH LANGUAGE. By R. G. LATHAM, M.A. M.D. Abridged from Dr. Latham's Edition of Johnson's English Dictionary, and condensed into One Volume. Medium 8vo. price 24s.

A DICTIONARY of the ENGLISH LANGUAGE. By R. G. LATHAM, M.A. M.D. Founded on the Dictionary of Dr. SAMUEL JOHNSON, as edited by the Rev. H. J. TODD, with numerous Emendations and Additions. In Four Volumes, 4to. price £7.

THESAURUS of ENGLISH WORDS and PHRASES, classified and arranged so as to facilitate the Expression of Ideas, and assist in Literary Composition. By P. M. ROGET, M.D. New Edition. Crown 8vo. 10s. 6d.

LECTURES on the SCIENCE of LANGUAGE. By F. MAX MÜLLER, M.A. &c. The Eighth Edition. 2 vols. crown 8vo. 16s.

MANUAL of ENGLISH LITERATURE, Historical and Critical. By THOMAS ARNOLD, M.A. New Edition. Crown 8vo. 7s. 6d.

SOUTHEY'S DOCTOR, complete in One Volume. Edited by the Rev. J. W. WARTER, B.D. Square crown 8vo. 12s. 6d.

HISTORICAL and CRITICAL COMMENTARY on the OLD TESTA-MENT; with a New Translation. By M. M. KALISCH, Ph.D. VOL. I. *Genesis,* 8vo. 18s. or adapted for the General Reader, 12s. VOL. II. *Exodus,* 15s. or adapted for the General Reader, 12s. VOL. III. *Leviticus,* PART I. 15s. or adapted for the General Reader, 8s. VOL. IV. *Leviticus,* PART II. 15s. or adapted for the General Reader, 8s.

A DICTIONARY of ROMAN and GREEK ANTIQUITIES, with about Two Thousand Engravings on Wood from Ancient Originals, illustrative of the Industrial Arts and Social Life of the Greeks and Romans. By A. RICH, B.A. Third Edition, revised and improved. Crown 8vo. price 7s. 6d.

A LATIN-ENGLISH DICTIONARY. By JOHN T. WHITE, D.D. Oxon. and J. E. RIDDLE, M.A. Oxon. Fifth Edition. 1 vol. 4to. 28s.

WHITE'S COLLEGE LATIN-ENGLISH DICTIONARY (Intermediate Size), abridged for the use of University Students from the Parent Work (as above). Medium 8vo. Third Edition, 15s.

WHITE'S JUNIOR STUDENT'S COMPLETE LATIN-ENGLISH and ENGLISH-LATIN DICTIONARY. New Edition. Square 12mo. price 12s.

Separately { The ENGLISH-LATIN DICTIONARY, price 5s. 6d.
{ The LATIN-ENGLISH DICTIONARY, price 7s. 6d.

A LATIN-ENGLISH DICTIONARY, adapted for the Use of Middle-Class Schools. By JOHN T. WHITE, D.D. Oxon. Square fcp. 8vo. price 3s.

An ENGLISH-GREEK LEXICON, containing all the Greek Words used by Writers of good authority. By C. D. YONGE, M.A. 4to. price 21s.

Mr. YONGE'S NEW LEXICON, English and Greek, abridged from his larger work (as above). Revised Edition. Square 12mo. price 8s. 6d.

A GREEK-ENGLISH LEXICON. Compiled by H. G. LIDDELL, D.D. Dean of Christ Church, and R. SCOTT, D.D. Dean of Rochester. Sixth Edition. Crown 4to. price 36s.

A LEXICON, GREEK and ENGLISH, abridged from LIDDELL and SCOTT'S *Greek-English Lexicon.* Fourteenth Edition. Square 12mo. 7s. 6d.

A PRACTICAL DICTIONARY of the FRENCH and ENGLISH LAN-GUAGES. By L. CONTANSEAU. Revised Edition. Post 8vo. 7s. 6d.

CONTANSEAU'S POCKET DICTIONARY, French and English, abridged from the above by the Author. New Edition. Square 18mo. 3s. 6d.

A NEW POCKET DICTIONARY of the GERMAN and ENGLISH
LANGUAGES. By F. W. LONGMAN, Balliol College, Oxford. 18mo. 5s.

NEW PRACTICAL DICTIONARY of the GERMAN LANGUAGE;
German-English and English-German. By the Rev. W. L. BLACKLEY, M.A.
and Dr. CARL MARTIN FRIEDLÄNDER. Post 8vo. 7s. 6d.

The MASTERY of LANGUAGES; or, the Art of Speaking Foreign
Tongues Idiomatically. By THOMAS PRENDERGAST. 8vo. 6s.

Miscellaneous Works and *Popular Metaphysics.*

LECTURES delivered in AMERICA in 1874. By CHARLES KINGSLEY,
F.L.S. F.G.S. late Rector of Eversley. Crown 8vo. price 5s.

GERMAN HOME LIFE. Reprinted, with Revision and Additions,
from *Fraser's Magazine.* Crown 8vo. 6s.

THE MISCELLANEOUS WORKS of THOMAS ARNOLD, D.D.
Late Head Master of Rugby School and Regius Professor of Modern History in
the University of Oxford, collected and republished. 8vo. 7s. 6d.

MISCELLANEOUS and POSTHUMOUS WORKS of the Late HENRY
THOMAS BUCKLE. Edited, with a Biographical Notice, by HELEN TAYLOR.
3 vols. 8vo. price 52s. 6d.

MISCELLANEOUS WRITINGS of JOHN CONINGTON, M.A. late
Corpus Professor of Latin in the University of Oxford. Edited by J. A.
SYMONDS, M.A. With a Memoir by H. J. S. SMITH, M.A. 2 vols. 8vo. 28s.

ESSAYS, CRITICAL and BIOGRAPHICAL. Contributed to the
Edinburgh Review. By HENRY ROGERS. New Edition, with Additions. 2 vols.
crown 8vo. price 12s.

ESSAYS on some THEOLOGICAL CONTROVERSIES of the TIME.
Contributed chiefly to the *Edinburgh Review.* By HENRY ROGERS. New
Edition, with Additions. Crown 8vo. price 6s.

RECREATIONS of a COUNTRY PARSON. By A. K. H. B. FIRST
and SECOND SERIES, crown 8vo. 3s. 6d. each.

The Common-place Philosopher in Town and Country. By A. K. H. B.
Crown 8vo. price 3s. 6d.

Leisure Hours in Town; Essays Consolatory, Æsthetical, Moral,
Social, and Domestic. By A. K. H. B. Crown 8vo. 3s. 6d.

The Autumn Holidays of a Country Parson; Essays contributed to
Fraser's Magazine, &c. By A. K. H. B. Crown 8vo. 3s. 6d.

Seaside Musings on Sundays and Week-Days. By A. K. H. B.
Crown 8vo. price 3s. 6d.

The Graver Thoughts of a Country Parson. By A. K. H. B. FIRST,
SECOND, and THIRD SERIES, crown 8vo. 3s. 6d. each.

Critical Essays of a Country Parson, selected from Essays contributed to *Fraser's Magazine.* By A. K. H. B. Crown 8vo. 3s. 6d.

Sunday Afternoons at the Parish Church of a Scottish University
City. By A. K. H. B. Crown 8vo. 3s. 6d.

Lessons of Middle Age; with some Account of various Cities and Men. By A. K. H. B. Crown 8vo. 3s. 6d.

Counsel and Comfort spoken from a City Pulpit. By A. K. H. B. Crown 8vo. price 3s. 6d.

Changed Aspects of Unchanged Truths; Memorials of St. Andrews Sundays. By A. K. H. B. Crown 8vo. 3s. 6d.

Present-day Thoughts; Memorials of St. Andrews Sundays. By A. K. H. B. Crown 8vo. 3s. 6d.

Landscapes, Churches, and Moralities. By A. K. H. B. Crown 8vo. price 3s. 6d.

SHORT STUDIES on GREAT SUBJECTS. By JAMES ANTHONY FROUDE, M.A. late Fellow of Exeter Coll. Oxford. 2 vols. crown 8vo. price 12s. or 2 vols. demy 8vo. price 24s.

SELECTIONS from the WRITINGS of LORD MACAULAY. Edited, with Occasional Explanatory Notes, by GEORGE OTTO TREVELYAN, M.P. 1 vol. crown 8vo.   [In the press.

LORD MACAULAY'S MISCELLANEOUS WRITINGS:—
            LIBRARY EDITION. 2 vols. 8vo. Portrait, 21s.
            PEOPLE'S EDITION. 1 vol. crown 8vo. 4s. 6d.

LORD MACAULAY'S MISCELLANEOUS WRITINGS and SPEECHES.
            STUDENT'S EDITION, in crown 8vo. price 6s.

The Rev. SYDNEY SMITH'S MISCELLANEOUS WORKS; including his Contributions to the *Edinburgh Review.* Crown 8vo. 6s.

The WIT and WISDOM of the Rev. SYDNEY SMITH; a Selection of the most memorable Passages in his Writings and Conversation. 16mo. 3s. 6d.

The ECLIPSE of FAITH; or, a Visit to a Religious Sceptic. By HENRY ROGERS. Latest Edition. Fcp. 8vo. price 5s.

Defence of the Eclipse of Faith, by its Author; a rejoinder to Dr. Newman's *Reply.* Latest Edition. Fcp 8vo. price 3s. 6d.

CHIPS from a GERMAN WORKSHOP; Essays on the Science of Religion, on Mythology, Traditions, and Customs, and on the Science of Language. By F. MAX MÜLLER, M.A. &c. 4 vols. 8vo. £2. 18s.

ANALYSIS of the PHENOMENA of the HUMAN MIND. By JAMES MILL. A New Edition, with Notes, Illustrative and Critical, by ALEXANDER BAIN, ANDREW FINDLATER, and GEORGE GROTE. Edited, with additional Notes, by JOHN STUART MILL. 2 vols. 8vo. price 28s.

An INTRODUCTION to MENTAL PHILOSOPHY, on the Inductive Method. By J. D. MORELL, M.A. LL.D. 8vo. 12s.

PHILOSOPHY WITHOUT ASSUMPTIONS. By the Rev. T. P. KIRKMAN, F.R.S. Rector of Croft, near Warrington. 8vo. 10s. 6d.

The SENSES and the INTELLECT. By ALEXANDER BAIN, M.D. Professor of Logic in the University of Aberdeen. Third Edition. 8vo. 15s.

The EMOTIONS and the WILL. By ALEXANDER BAIN, LL.D. Professor of Logic in the University of Aberdeen. Third Edition, thoroughly revised, and in great part re-written. 8vo. price 15s.

MENTAL and MORAL SCIENCE: a Compendium of Psychology and Ethics. By the same Author. Third Edition. Crown 8vo. 10s. 6d. Or separately: PART I. *Mental Science,* 6s. 6d. PART II. *Moral Science,* 4s. 6d.

LOGIC, DEDUCTIVE and INDUCTIVE. By ALEXANDER BAIN, LL.D.
In TWO PARTS, crown 8vo. 10s. 6d. Each Part may be had separately :—
PART I. *Deduction*, 4s. PART II. *Induction*, 6s. 6d.

A BUDGET of PARADOXES. By AUGUSTUS DE MORGAN, **F.R.A.S.**
and C.P.S. 8vo. 15s.

APPARITIONS; a Narrative of Facts. By the Rev. B. W. SAVILE,
M.A. Author of 'The Truth of the Bible' &c. Crown 8vo. price 4s. 6d.

A TREATISE of HUMAN NATURE, being an Attempt to Introduce
the Experimental Method of Reasoning into Moral Subjects; followed by Dia-
logues concerning Natural Religion. By DAVID HUME. Edited, with Notes,
&c. by T. H. GREEN, Fellow and Tutor, Ball. Coll. and T. H. GROSE, Fellow
and Tutor, Queen's Coll. Oxford. 2 vols. 8vo. 28s.

ESSAYS MORAL, POLITICAL, and LITERARY. By DAVID HUME.
By the same Editors. 2 vols. 8vo. price 28s.

The PHILOSOPHY of NECESSITY; or, Natural Law as applicable to
Mental, Moral, and Social Science. By CHARLES BRAY. 8vo. 9s.

UEBERWEG'S SYSTEM of LOGIC and HISTORY of LOGICAL
DOCTRINES. Translated, with Notes and Appendices, by T. M. LINDSAY,
M.A. F.R.S.E. 8vo. price 16s.

FRAGMENTARY PAPERS on SCIENCE and other Subjects. By
the late Sir H. HOLLAND, Bart. Edited by his Son, the Rev. F. HOLLAND, 8vo.
price 14s.

Astronomy, Meteorology, Popular Geography, &c.

BRINKLEY'S ASTRONOMY. Revised and partly re-written, with
Additional Chapters, and an Appendix of Questions for Examination. By J. W.
STUBBS, D.D. Fellow and Tutor of Trinity College, Dublin, and F. BRUNNOW,
Ph.D. Astronomer Royal of Ireland. Crown 8vo. price 6s.

OUTLINES of ASTRONOMY. By Sir J. F. W. HERSCHEL, Bart.
M.A. Latest Edition, with Plates and Diagrams. Square crown 8vo. 12s.

ESSAYS on ASTRONOMY, a Series of Papers on Planets and Meteors,
the Sun and Sun-surrounding Space, Stars and Star-Cloudlets; with a Dissertation
on the Transit of Venus. By R. A. PROCTOR, B.A. With Plates and Woodcuts. 8vo. 12s.

THE TRANSITS of VENUS; a Popular Account of Past and Coming
Transits, from the first observed by Horrocks A.D. 1639 to the Transit of
A.D. 2012. By R. A. PROCTOR, B.A. Second Edition, with 20 Plates (12 coloured)
and 38 Woodcuts. Crown 8vo. 8s. 6d.

The UNIVERSE and the COMING TRANSITS : Presenting Researches into and New Views respecting the Constitution of the Heavens;
together with an Investigation of the Conditions of the Coming Transits of Venus.
By R. A. PROCTOR, B.A. With 22 Charts and 22 Woodcuts. 8vo. 16s.

The MOON; her Motions, Aspect, Scenery, and Physical Condition.
By R. A. PROCTOR, B.A. With Plates, Charts, Woodcuts, and Three Lunar
Photographs. Crown 8vo. 15s.

The SUN; RULER, LIGHT, FIRE, and LIFE of the PLANETARY
SYSTEM. By R. A. PROCTOR, B.A. Second Edition, with 10 Plates (7 coloured) and 107 Figures on Wood. Crown 8vo. 14s.

OTHER WORLDS THAN OURS; the Plurality of Worlds Studied
under the Light of Recent Scientific Researches. By R. A. PROCTOR, B.A.
Third Edition, with 14 Illustrations. **Crown 8vo. 10s. 6d.**

The ORBS AROUND US; Familiar Essays on the Moon and Planets,
Meteors and **Comets, the** Sun and Coloured **Pairs of** Stars. By R. A. PROCTOR,
B.A. Second Edition, with Charts and 4 Diagrams. Crown 8vo. price 7s. 6d.

SATURN and its SYSTEM. By R. A. PROCTOR, B.A. 8vo. with 14
Plates, 14s.

The MOON, and the Condition and Configurations of its Surface.
By EDMUND NEISON, Fellow of the Royal Astronomical Society, &c. With 26
Maps and 5 Plates. Medium 8vo. 31s. 6d.

A NEW STAR ATLAS, for the Library, the School, and the Observatory,
in Twelve Circular Maps (with Two Index Plates). Intended as a Companion
to 'Webb's Celestial Objects for Common Telescopes.' With a Letterpress
Introduction on the Study of the Stars, illustrated by 9 Diagrams. By R. A.
PROCTOR, B.A. Crown 8vo. 5s.

SCHELLEN'S SPECTRUM ANALYSIS, in its application to Terrestrial **Substances** and the Physical Constitution of the Heavenly Bodies. Translated by JANE and C. LASSELL; edited, with Notes, by W. HUGGINS, LL.D.
F.R.S. With 13 Plates (6 coloured) and 223 Woodcuts. 8vo. price 28s.

CELESTIAL OBJECTS for COMMON TELESCOPES. By the Rev.
T. W. WEBB, M.A. F.R.A.S. Third Edition, revised and enlarged; with Maps,
Plate, and Woodcuts. Crown 8vo. price 7s. 6d.

AIR and RAIN; the Beginnings of a Chemical Climatology. By
ROBERT ANGUS SMITH, Ph.D. F.R.S. F.C.S. With 8 Illustrations. 8vo. 24s.

AIR and its RELATIONS to LIFE; being, with some Additions,
the Substance of a Course of Lectures delivered at the Royal Institution of
Great Britain. By W. N. HARTLEY, F.C.S. Demonstrator of Chemistry at King's
College, London. Second Edition, with 66 Woodcuts. Small 8vo. 6s.

NAUTICAL SURVEYING, an INTRODUCTION to the PRACTICAL
and THEORETICAL STUDY of. By J. K. LAUGHTON, M.A. Small 8vo. 6s.

DOVE'S LAW of STORMS, considered in connexion with the Ordinary
Movements of the Atmosphere. Translated by R. H. SCOTT, M.A. 8vo. 10s. 6d.

KEITH JOHNSTON'S GENERAL DICTIONARY of GEOGRAPHY,
Descriptive, Physical, Statistical, and Historical; forming a complete Gazetteer
of the World. New Edition, revised and corrected. 1 vol. 8vo. [Nearly ready.

The PUBLIC SCHOOLS ATLAS of MODERN GEOGRAPHY. In 31
Coloured Maps, exhibiting clearly the more important Physical Features of the
Countries delineated, and Noting all the Chief Places of Historical, Commercial,
or Social Interest. Edited, with an Introduction, by the Rev. G. BUTLER, M.A.
Imperial 8vo. or imperial 4to. 5s. cloth.

The PUBLIC SCHOOLS MANUAL of MODERN GEOGRAPHY. By
the Rev. GEORGE BUTLER, M.A. Principal of Liverpool College; Editor of 'The
Public Schools Atlas of Modern Geography.'   [In preparation.

The PUBLIC SCHOOLS ATLAS of ANCIENT GEOGRAPHY, in 25
Coloured Maps. Edited by the Rev. GEORGE BUTLER, M.A. Principal of
Liverpool College. Imperial 8vo. or imperial 4to. 7s. 6d. cloth.

MAUNDER'S TREASURY of GEOGRAPHY, Physical, Historical,
Descriptive, and Political. Edited by W. HUGHES, F.R.G.S. Revised Edition,
with 7 Maps and 16 Plates. Fcp. 6s. cloth, or 10s. 6d. bound in calf.

Natural History and *Popular Science.*

TEXT-BOOKS of SCIENCE, MECHANICAL and PHYSICAL, adapted for the use of Artisans and of Students in Public and Science Schools.

The following Text-Books in this Series may now be had :—

ANDERSON'S Strength of Materials, small 8vo. 3*s.* 6*d.*
ARMSTRONG'S Organic Chemistry, 3*s.* 6*d.*
BARRY'S Railway Appliances, 3*s.* 6*d.*
BLOXAM'S Metals, 3*s.* 6*d.*
GOODEVE'S Elements of Mechanism, 3*s.* 6*d.*
———— Principles of Mechanics, 3*s.* 6*d.*
GRIFFIN'S Algebra and Trigonometry, 3*s.* 6*d.* Notes, 3*s.*6*d.*
JENKIN'S Electricity and Magnetism, 3*s.* 6*d.*
MAXWELL'S Theory of Heat, 3*s.* 6*d.*
MERRIFIELD'S Technical Arithmetic and Mensuration, 3*s.* 6*d.* Key, 3*s.* 6*d.*
MILLER'S Inorganic Chemistry, 3*s.* 6*d.*
PREECE & SIVEWRIGHT'S Telegraphy, 3*s.* 6*d.*
SHELLEY'S Workshop Appliances, 3*s.* 6*d.*
THORPE'S Quantitative Chemical Analysis, 4*s.* 6*d.*
THORPE & MUIR'S Qualitative Analysis, 3*s.* 6*d.*
TILDEN'S Chemical Philosophy, 3*s.* 6*d.*
WATSON'S Plane and Solid Geometry, 3*s.* 6*d.*

*** Other Text-Books in extension of this Series are in active preparation.

ELEMENTARY TREATISE on PHYSICS, Experimental and Applied. Translated and edited from GANOT'S *Éléments de Physique* by E. ATKINSON, Ph.D. F.C.S. Seventh Edition, revised and enlarged ; with 4 Coloured Plates and 758 Woodcuts. Post 8vo. 15*s.*

NATURAL PHILOSOPHY for GENERAL READERS and YOUNG PERSONS ; being a Course of Physics divested of Mathematical Formulæ expressed in the language of daily life. Translated from GANOT'S *Cours de Physique* and by E. ATKINSON, Ph.D. F.C.S. Second Edition, with 2 Plates and 429 Woodcuts. Crown 8vo. price 7*s.* 6*d.*

HELMHOLTZ'S POPULAR LECTURES on SCIENTIFIC SUBJECTS. Translated by E. ATKINSON, Ph.D. F.C.S. Professor of Experimental Science, Staff College. With an Introduction by Professor TYNDALL. 8vo. with numerous Woodcuts, price 12*s.* 6*d.*

On the SENSATIONS of TONE as a Physiological Basis for the Theory of Music. By HERMANN L. F. HELMHOLTZ, M.D. Professor of Physics in the University of Berlin. Translated, with the Author's sanction, from the Third German Edition, with Additional Notes and an Additional Appendix, by ALEXANDER J. ELLIS, F.R.S. &c. 8vo. price 36*s.*

The HISTORY of MODERN MUSIC, a Course of Lectures delivered at the Royal Institution of Great Britain. By JOHN HULLAH, Professor of Vocal Music in Queen's College and Bedford College, and Organist of Charterhouse. New Edition. 8vo. 8*s.* 6*d.*

The TRANSITION PERIOD of MUSICAL HISTORY; a Second Course of Lectures on the History of Music from the Beginning of the Seventeenth to the Middle of the Eighteenth Century, delivered at the Royal Institution. By JOHN HULLAH. New Edition. 8vo. 10*s.* 6*d.*

SOUND. By JOHN TYNDALL, LL.D. D.C.L. F.R.S. Third Edition, including Recent Researches on Fog-Signalling ; Portrait and Woodcuts. Crown 8vo. 10*s.* 6*d.*

HEAT a MODE of MOTION. By JOHN TYNDALL, LL.D. D.C.L. F.R.S. Fifth Edition. Plate and Woodcuts. Crown 8vo. 10*s.* 6*d.*

CONTRIBUTIONS to MOLECULAR PHYSICS in the DOMAIN of RADIANT HEAT. By J. Tyndall, LL.D. D.C.L. F.R.S. With 2 Plates and 31 Woodcuts. 8vo. 16s.

RESEARCHES on DIAMAGNETISM and MAGNE-CRYSTALLIC ACTION; including the Question of Diamagnetic Polarity. By J. Tyndall, M.D. D.C.L. F.R.S. With 6 plates and many Woodcuts. 8vo. 14s.

NOTES of a COURSE of SEVEN LECTURES on ELECTRICAL PHENOMENA and THEORIES, delivered at the Royal Institution, A.D. 1870. By John Tyndall, LL.D., D.C.L., F.R.S. Crown 8vo. 1s. sewed; 1s. 6d. cloth.

SIX LECTURES on LIGHT delivered in America in 1872 and 1873. By John Tyndall, LL.D. D.C.L. F.R.S. Second Edition, with Portrait, Plate, and 59 Diagrams. Crown 8vo. 7s. 6d.

NOTES of a COURSE of NINE LECTURES on LIGHT delivered at the Royal Institution, A.D. 1869. By John Tyndall, LL.D. D.C.L. F.R.S. Crown 8vo. price 1s. sewed, or 1s. 6d. cloth.

FRAGMENTS of SCIENCE. By John Tyndall, LL.D. D.C.L. F.R.S. Third Edition, with a New Introduction. Crown 8vo. 10s. 6d.

LIGHT SCIENCE for LEISURE HOURS; a Series of Familiar Essays on Scientific Subjects, Natural Phenomena, &c. By R. A. Proctor, B.A. First and Second Series. Crown 8vo. 7s. 6d. each.

A TREATISE on MAGNETISM, General and Terrestrial. By Humphrey Lloyd, D.D. D.C.L., Provost of Trinity College, Dublin. 8vo. 10s. 6d.

ELEMENTARY TREATISE on the WAVE-THEORY of LIGHT. By Humphrey Lloyd, D.D. D.C.L. Provost of Trinity College, Dublin. Third Edition, revised and enlarged. 8vo. price 10s. 6d.

The CORRELATION of PHYSICAL FORCES. By the Hon. Sir W. R. Grove, M.A. F.R.S. one of the Judges of the Court of Common Pleas. Sixth Edition, with other Contributions to Science. 8vo. price 15s.

The COMPARATIVE ANATOMY and PHYSIOLOGY of the VERTE- BRATE ANIMALS. By Richard Owen, F.R.S. D.C.L. With 1,472 Woodcuts. 3 vols. 8vo. £3. 13s. 6d.

PRINCIPLES of ANIMAL MECHANICS. By the Rev. S. Haughton, F.R.S. Fellow of Trin. Coll. Dubl. M.D. Dubl. and D.C.L. Oxon. Second Edition, with 111 Figures on Wood. 8vo. 21s.

ROCKS CLASSIFIED and DESCRIBED. By Bernhard Von Cotta. English Edition, by P. H. Lawrence; with English, German, and French Synonymes. Post 8vo. 14s.

The ANCIENT STONE IMPLEMENTS, WEAPONS, and ORNA- MENTS of GREAT BRITAIN. By John Evans, F.R.S. F.S.A. With 2 Plates and 476 Woodcuts. 8vo. price 28s.

The NATIVE RACES of the PACIFIC STATES of NORTH AMERICA. By Hubert Howe Bancroft. 5 vols. 8vo. with Maps, £6. 5s.

The ORIGIN of CIVILISATION and the PRIMITIVE CONDITION of MAN ; Mental and Social Condition of Savages. By Sir John Lubbock, Bart. M.P. F.R.S. Third Edition, with 25 Woodcuts. 8vo. 18s.

BIBLE ANIMALS; being a Description of every Living Creature mentioned in the Scriptures, from the Ape to the Coral. By the Rev. J. G. Wood, M.A. F.L.S. With about 112 Vignettes on Wood. 8vo. 14s.

HOMES WITHOUT HANDS; a Description of the Habitations of Animals, classed according to their Principle of Construction. By the Rev. J. G. WOOD, M.A. F.L.S. With about 140 Vignettes on Wood. 8vo. 14s.

INSECTS AT HOME; a Popular Account of British Insects, their Structure, Habits, and Transformations. By the Rev. J. G. WOOD, M.A. F.L.S. With upwards of 700 Illustrations. 8vo. price 14s.

INSECTS ABROAD; a Popular Account of Foreign Insects, their Structure, Habits, and Transformations. By J. G. WOOD, M.A. F.L.S. Printed and illustrated uniformly with 'Insects at Home.' 8vo. price 21s.

STRANGE DWELLINGS; a description of the Habitations of Animals, abridged from 'Homes without Hands.' By the Rev. J. G. WOOD, M.A. F.L.S. With about 60 Woodcut Illustrations. Crown 8vo. price 7s. 6d.

OUT of DOORS; a Selection of original Articles on Practical Natural History. By the Rev. J. G. WOOD, M.A. F.L.S. With Eleven Illustrations from Original Designs engraved on Wood by G. Pearson. Crown 8vo. price 7s. 6d.

A FAMILIAR HISTORY of BIRDS. By E. STANLEY, D.D. F.R.S. late Lord Bishop of Norwich. Seventh Edition, with Woodcuts. Fcp. 3s. 6d.

The SEA and its LIVING WONDERS. By Dr. GEORGE HARTWIG. Latest revised Edition. 8vo. with many Illustrations, 10s. 6d.

The TROPICAL WORLD. By Dr. GEORGE HARTWIG. With above 160 Illustrations. Latest revised Edition. 8vo. price 10s. 6d.

The SUBTERRANEAN WORLD. By Dr. GEORGE HARTWIG. With 3 Maps and about 80 Woodcuts, including 8 full size of page. 8vo. price 10s. 6d.

The POLAR WORLD, a Popular Description of Man and Nature in the Arctic and Antarctic Regions of the Globe. By Dr. GEORGE HARTWIG. With 8 Chromoxylographs, 3 Maps, and 85 Woodcuts. 8vo. 10s. 6d.

THE AERIAL WORLD. By Dr. G. HARTWIG. New Edition, with 8 Chromoxylographs and 60 Woodcut Illustrations. 8vo. price 21s.

KIRBY and SPENCE'S INTRODUCTION to ENTOMOLOGY, or Elements of the Natural History of Insects. 7th Edition. Crown 8vo. 5s.

MAUNDER'S TREASURY of NATURAL HISTORY, or Popular Dictionary of Birds, Beasts, Fishes, Reptiles, Insects, and Creeping Things. With above 900 Woodcuts. Fcp. 8vo. price 6s. cloth, or 10s. 6d. bound in calf.

MAUNDER'S SCIENTIFIC and LITERARY TREASURY. New Edition, thoroughly revised and in great part rewritten, with above 1,000 new Articles, by J. Y. JOHNSON. Fcp. 8vo. 6s. cloth, or 10s. 6d. calf.

BRANDE'S DICTIONARY of SCIENCE, LITERATURE, and ART. Re-edited by the Rev. GEORGE W. COX, M.A. late Scholar of Trinity College, Oxford; assisted by Contributors of eminent Scientific and Literary Acquirements. New Edition, revised. 3 vols. medium 8vo. 63s.

HANDBOOK of HARDY TREES, SHRUBS, and HERBACEOUS PLANTS, containing Descriptions, Native Countries, &c. of a Selection of the Best Species in Cultivation; together with Cultural Details, Comparative Hardiness, Suitability for Particular Positions, &c. By W. B. HEMSLEY. Based on DECAISNE and NAUDIN'S *Manuel de l'Amateur des Jardins*, and including the 264 Original Woodcuts. Medium 8vo. 21s.

A GENERAL SYSTEM of BOTANY DESCRIPTIVE and ANALYTICAL.
By E. Le Maout, and J. Decaisne, Members of the Institute of France.
Translated by Mrs. Hooker. The Orders arranged after the Method followed
in the Universities and Schools of Great Britain, its Colonies, America, and
India; with an Appendix on the Natural Method, and other Additions, by
J. D. Hooker, F.R.S. &c. Second Thousand, with 5,500 Woodcuts. Imperial
8vo. 31s. 6d.

The TREASURY of BOTANY, or Popular Dictionary of the Vegetable
Kingdom; including a Glossary of Botanical Terms. Edited by J. Lindley,
F.R.S. and T. Moore, F.L.S. assisted by eminent Contributors. With 274
Woodcuts and 20 Steel Plates. Two Parts, fcp. 8vo. 12s. cloth, or 21s. calf.

The ELEMENTS of BOTANY for FAMILIES and SCHOOLS.
Tenth Edition, revised by Thomas Moore, F.L.S. Fcp. 8vo. with 154 Woodcuts, 2s. 6d.

The ROSE AMATEUR'S GUIDE. By Thomas Rivers. Fourteenth
Edition. Fcp. 8vo. 4s.

LOUDON'S ENCYCLOPÆDIA of PLANTS; comprising the Specific
Character, Description, Culture, History, &c. of all the Plants found in
Great Britain. With upwards of 12,000 Woodcuts. 8vo. 42s.

FOREST TREES and WOODLAND SCENERY, as described in Ancient
and Modern Poets. By William Menzies, Deputy Surveyor of Windsor Forest
and Parks, &c. With Twenty Chromo-lithographic Plates. Folio, price £5 5s.

Chemistry and *Physiology.*

A DICTIONARY of CHEMISTRY and the Allied Branches of other
Sciences. By Henry Watts, F.R.S. assisted by eminent Contributors.
Seven Volumes, medium 8vo. price £10, 16s. 6d.

ELEMENTS of CHEMISTRY, Theoretical and Practical. By W. Allen
Miller, M.D. late Prof. of Chemistry, King's Coll. London. New
Edition. 3 vols. 8vo. Part I. Chemical Physics, 15s. Part II.
Inorganic Chemistry, 21s. Part III. Organic Chemistry, New Edition
in the press.

SELECT METHODS in CHEMICAL ANALYSIS, chiefly INOR-
GANIC. By William Crookes, F.R.S. With 22 Woodcuts. Crown 8vo.
price 12s. 6d.

A PRACTICAL HANDBOOK of DYEING and CALICO PRINTING.
By William Crookes, F.R.S. With 11 Page Plates, 49 Specimens of Dyed and
Printed Fabrics, and 36 Woodcuts. 8vo. 42s.

OUTLINES of PHYSIOLOGY, Human and Comparative. By John
Marshall, F.R.C.S. Surgeon to the University College Hospital. 2 vols.
crown 8vo. with 122 Woodcuts, 32s.

HEALTH in the HOUSE; a Series of Lectures on Elementary Physiology in its application to the Daily Wants of Man and Animals, delivered to
the Wives and Children of Working Men in Leeds and Saltaire. By Catherine
M. Buckton. New Edition, revised. Small 8vo. Woodcuts, 2s.

The Fine Arts, and *Illustrated Editions.*

A DICTIONARY of ARTISTS of the ENGLISH SCHOOL: Painters, Sculptors, Architects, Engravers, and Ornamentists ; with Notices of their Lives and Works. By S. REDGRAVE. 8vo. 16s.

MOORE'S IRISH MELODIES, with 161 Steel Plates from Original Drawings by D. MACLISE, R.A. Super-royal 8vo. 21s.

LORD MACAULAY'S LAYS of ANCIENT ROME. With 90 Illustrations on Wood, from the Antique, from Drawings by G. SCHARF. Fcp. 4to. 21s.

Miniature Edition of Lord Macaulay's Lays of Ancient Rome, with the Illustrations (as above) reduced in Lithography. Imp. 16mo. 10s. 6d.

POEMS. By WILLIAM B. SCOTT. I. Ballads and Tales. II. Studies from Nature. III. Sonnets &c. Illustrated by 17 Etchings by W. B. SCOTT (the Author) and L. ALMA TADEMA. Crown 8vo. price 15s.

HALF-HOUR LECTURES on the HISTORY and PRACTICE of the FINE and ORNAMENTAL ARTS. By WILLIAM B. SCOTT. Third Edition, with 50 Woodcuts. Crown 8vo. 8s. 6d.

The THREE CATHEDRALS DEDICATED to ST. PAUL, in LONDON ; their History from the Foundation of the First Building in the Sixth Century to the Proposals for the Adornment of the Present Cathedral. By WILLIAM LONGMAN, F.A.S. With numerous Illustrations. Square crown 8vo. 21s.

IN FAIRYLAND ; Pictures from the Elf-World. By RICHARD DOYLE. With a Poem by W. ALLINGHAM. With Sixteen Plates, containing Thirty-six Designs printed in Colours. Second Edition. Folio, price 15s.

The NEW TESTAMENT, illustrated with Wood Engravings after the Early Masters, chiefly of the Italian School. Crown 4to. 63s. cloth, gilt top ; or £5 5s. elegantly bound in morocco.

SACRED and LEGENDARY ART. By MRS. JAMESON.

Legends of the Saints and Martyrs. New Edition, with 19 Etchings and 187 Woodcuts. 2 vols. square crown 8vo. 31s. 6d.

Legends of the Monastic Orders. New Edition, with 11 Etchings and 88 Woodcuts. 1 vol. square crown 8vo. 21s.

Legends of the Madonna. New Edition, with 27 Etchings and 165 Woodcuts. 1 vol. square crown 8vo. 21s.

The History of Our Lord, with that of his Types and Precursors. Completed by Lady EASTLAKE. Revised Edition, with 31 Etchings and 281 Woodcuts. 2 vols. square crown 8vo. 42s.

The Useful Arts, Manufactures, &c.

GWILT'S ENCYCLOPÆDIA of ARCHITECTURE, with above 1,600 Engravings on Wood. New Edition, revised and enlarged by WYATT PAPWORTH. 8vo. 52s. 6d.

HINTS on HOUSEHOLD TASTE in FURNITURE, UPHOLSTERY, and other Details. By CHARLES L. EASTLAKE, Architect. New Edition, with about 90 Illustrations. Square crown 8vo. 14s.

B

INDUSTRIAL CHEMISTRY; a Manual for Manufacturers and for use in Colleges or Technical Schools. Being a Translation of Professors Stohmann and Engler's German Edition of PAYEN's *Précis de Chimie Industrielle*, by Dr. J. D. BARRY. Edited and supplemented by B. H. PAUL, Ph.D. 8vo. with Plates and Woodcuts. [*In the press.*

URE'S DICTIONARY of ARTS, MANUFACTURES, and MINES. Seventh Edition, rewritten and enlarged by ROBERT HUNT, F.R.S. assisted by numerous Contributors eminent in Science and the Arts, and familiar with Manufactures. With above 2,100 Woodcuts. 3 vols. medium 8vo. £5 5s.

HANDBOOK of PRACTICAL TELEGRAPHY. By R. S. CULLEY Memb. Inst. C.E. Engineer-in-Chief of Telegraphs to the Post Office. Sixth Edition, with 144 Woodcuts and 5 Plates. 8vo. price 16s.

TELEGRAPHY. By W. H. PREECE, C.E. Divisional Engineer, P.O. Telegraphs; and J. SIVEWRIGHT, M.A. Superintendent (Engineering Department) P.O. Telegraphs. Small 8vo. with 160 Woodcuts, 3s. 6d.

RAILWAY APPLIANCES; a Description of Details of Railway Construction subsequent to the completion of the Earthworks and Masonry, including a short Notice of Railway Rolling Stock. By J. W. BARRY, Member of the Institution of Civil Engineers. Small 8vo. with 207 Woodcuts, 3s. 6d.

ENCYCLOPÆDIA of CIVIL ENGINEERING, Historical, Theoretical, and Practical. By E. CRESY, C.E. With above 3,000 Woodcuts. 8vo. 42s.

OCCASIONAL PAPERS on SUBJECTS connected with CIVIL ENGINEERING, GUNNERY, and Naval Architecture. By MICHAEL SCOTT, Memb. Inst. C.E. & of Inst. N.A. 2 vols. 8vo. with Plates, 42s.

NAVAL POWERS and their POLICY, with Tabular Statements of British and Foreign Ironclad Navies, giving Dimensions, Armour, Details of Armament, Engines, Speed, &c. By JOHN C. PAGET. 8vo. 10s. 6d.

TREATISE on MILLS and MILLWORK. By Sir W. FAIRBAIRN, Bart. F.R.S. New Edition, with 18 Plates and 322 Woodcuts, 2 vols. 8vo. 32s.

USEFUL INFORMATION for ENGINEERS. By Sir W. FAIRBAIRN, Bart. F.R.S. Revised Edition, with Illustrations. 3 vols. crown 8vo. price 31s. 6d.

The APPLICATION of CAST and WROUGHT IRON to Building Purposes. By Sir W. FAIRBAIRN, Bart. F.R.S. Fourth Edition, enlarged; with 6 Plates and 118 Woodcuts. 8vo. price 16s.

The THEORY of STRAINS in GIRDERS and similar Structures, with Observations on the application of Theory to Practice, and Tables of the Strength and other Properties of Materials. By BINDON B. STONEY, M.A. M. Inst. C.E. New Edition, royal 8vo. with 5 Plates and 123 Woodcuts, 36s.

A TREATISE on the STEAM ENGINE, in its various Applications to Mines, Mills, Steam Navigation, Railways, and Agriculture. By J. BOURNE, C.E. Eighth Edition; with Portrait, 37 Plates, and 546 Woodcuts. 4to. 42s.

CATECHISM of the STEAM ENGINE, in its various Applications to Mines, Mills, Steam Navigation, Railways, and Agriculture. By the same Author. With 89 Woodcuts. Fcp. 8vo. 6s.

HANDBOOK of the STEAM ENGINE. By the same Author, forming a KEY to the Catechism of the Steam Engine, with 67 Woodcuts. Fcp. 9s.

BOURNE'S RECENT IMPROVEMENTS in the STEAM ENGINE in its various applications to Mines, Mills, Steam Navigation, Railways, and Agriculture. By JOHN BOURNE, C.E. New Edition, with 124 Woodcuts. Fcp. 8vo. 6s.

PRACTICAL TREATISE on METALLURGY, adapted from the last German Edition of Professor KERL's *Metallurgy* by W. CROOKES, F.R.S. &c. and E. BÖHRIG, Ph.D. M.E. With 625 Woodcuts. 3 vols. 8vo. price £4 19s.

MITCHELL'S MANUAL of PRACTICAL ASSAYING. Fourth Edition, for the most part rewritten, with all the recent Discoveries incorporated, by W. CROOKES, F.R.S. With 199 Woodcuts. 8vo. 31s. 6d.

LOUDON'S ENCYCLOPÆDIA of AGRICULTURE: comprising the Laying-out, Improvement, and Management of Landed Property, and the Cultivation and Economy of Agricultural Produce. With 1,100 Woodcuts. 8vo. 21s.

Loudon's Encyclopædia of Gardening: comprising the Theory and Practice of Horticulture, Floriculture, Arboriculture, and Landscape Gardening. With 1,000 Woodcuts. 8vo. 21s.

REMINISCENCES of FEN and MERE. By J. M. HEATHCOTE. With 27 Illustrations and 3 Maps. Square crown 8vo. price 28s.

Religious and *Moral Works.*

CHRISTIAN LIFE, its COURSE, its HINDRANCES, and its HELPS; Sermons preached mostly in the Chapel of Rugby School. By the late Rev. THOMAS ARNOLD, D.D. 8vo. 7s. 6d.

CHRISTIAN LIFE, its HOPES, its FEARS, and its CLOSE; Sermons preached mostly in the Chapel of Rugby School. By the late Rev. THOMAS ARNOLD, D.D. 8vo. 7s. 6d.

SERMONS chiefly on the INTERPRETATION of SCRIPTURE. By the late Rev. THOMAS ARNOLD, D.D. 8vo. price 7s. 6d.

SERMONS preached in the Chapel of Rugby School; with an Address before Confirmation. By the late Rev. THOMAS ARNOLD, D.D. Fcp. 8vo. 3s. 6d.

THREE ESSAYS on RELIGION: Nature; the Utility of Religion; Theism. By JOHN STUART MILL. 8vo. price 10s. 6d.

INTRODUCTION to the SCIENCE of RELIGION. Four Lectures delivered at the Royal Institution; with Two Essays on False Analogies and the Philosophy of Mythology. By F. MAX MÜLLER, M.A. Crown 8vo. 10s. 6d.

SUPERNATURAL RELIGION; an Inquiry into the Reality of Divine Revelation. Sixth Edition, carefully revised, with Eighty Pages of New Preface. 2 vols. 8vo. 24s.

NOTES on the EARLIER HEBREW SCRIPTURES. By Sir G. B. AIRY, K.C.B. 8vo. price 6s.

ISLAM under the ARABS. By ROBERT DRURIE OSBORN, Major in the Bengal Staff Corps. 8vo. 12s.

RELIGION and SCIENCE, their Relations to each other at the Present Day; Three Essays on the Grounds of Religious Beliefs. By STANLEY T. GIBSON, B.D. late Fellow of Queen's College, Cambridge. 8vo. 10s. 6d.

The PRIMITIVE and CATHOLIC FAITH in Relation to the Church of England. By the Rev. B. W. SAVILE, M.A. Rector of Shillingford, Exeter, Author of 'Truth of the Bible' &c. 8vo. price 7s.

SYNONYMS of the OLD TESTAMENT, their BEARING on CHRISTIAN FAITH and PRACTICE. By the Rev. R. B. GIRDLESTONE, M.A. 8vo. 15s.

An INTRODUCTION to the THEOLOGY of the CHURCH of ENGLAND, in an Exposition of the Thirty-nine Articles. By the Rev. T. P. BOULTBEE, LL.D. New Edition, Fcp. 8vo. price 6s.

An EXPOSITION of the 39 ARTICLES, Historical and Doctrinal. By E. HAROLD BROWNE, D.D. Lord Bishop of Winchester. New Edit. 8vo. 16s.

The LIFE and EPISTLES of ST. PAUL. By the Rev. W. J. CONYBEARE, M.A., and the Very Rev. J. S. HOWSON, D.D. Dean of Chester :—

LIBRARY EDITION, with all the Original Illustrations, Maps, Landscapes on Steel, Woodcuts, &c. 2 vols. 4to. 42s.

INTERMEDIATE EDITION, with a Selection of Maps, Plates, and Woodcuts. 2 vols. square crown 8vo. 21s.

STUDENT'S EDITION, revised and condensed, with 46 Illustrations and Maps. 1 vol. crown 8vo. price 9s.

HISTORY of the REFORMATION in EUROPE in the TIME of CALVIN. By the Rev. J. H. MERLE D'AUBIGNÉ, D.D. Translated by W. L. R. CATES. 7 vols. 8vo. price £5, 11s.
      *** Vol. VIII. completing the Work, is preparing for publication.

NEW TESTAMENT COMENTARIES. By the Rev. W. A. O'CONOR. B.A. Rector of St. Simon and St. Jude, Manchester. Crown 8vo.

> **Epistle to the Romans,** price 3s. 6d.
>
> **Epistle to the Hebrews,** 4s. 6d.
>
> **St. John's Gospel,** 10s. 6d.

A CRITICAL and GRAMMATICAL COMMENTARY on ST. PAUL'S Epistles. By C. J. ELLICOTT, D.D. Lord Bishop of Gloucester and Bristol. 8vo.

Galatians, Fourth Edition, 8s. 6d.

Ephesians, Fourth Edition, 8s. 6d.

Pastoral Epistles, Fourth Edition, 10s. 6d.

Philippians, Colossians, and Philemon, Third Edition, 10s. 6d.

Thessalonians, Third Edition, 7s. 6d.

HISTORICAL LECTURES on the LIFE of OUR LORD. By C. J. ELLICOTT, D.D. Bishop of Gloucester and Bristol. Sixth Edition. 8vo. 12s.

EVIDENCE of the TRUTH of the CHRISTIAN RELIGION derived from the Literal Fulfilment of Prophecy. By ALEXANDER KEITH, D.D. 37th Edition, with Plates, in square 8vo. 12s. 6d.; 39th Edition, in post 8vo. 6s.

HISTORY of ISRAEL. By H. EWALD, late Professor of the Univ. of Göttingen. Translated by J. E. CARPENTER, M.A., with a Preface by RUSSELL MARTINEAU, M.A. 5 vols. 8vo. 63s.

The ANTIQUITIES of ISRAEL. By HEINRICH EWALD, late Professor of the University of Göttingen. Translated from the German by HENRY SHAEN SOLLY, M.A. 8vo. price 12s. 6d.

The TREASURY of BIBLE KNOWLEDGE; being a Dictionary of the Books, Persons, Places, Events, and other matters of which mention is made in Holy Scripture. By Rev. J. AYRE, M.A. With Maps, 16 Plates, and numerous Woodcuts. Fcp. 8vo. price 6s. cloth, or 10s. 6d. neatly bound in calf.

LECTURES on the PENTATEUCH and the MOABITE STONE. By the Right Rev. J. W. Colenso, D.D. Bishop of Natal. 8vo. 12s.

The PENTATEUCH and BOOK of JOSHUA CRITICALLY EXAMINED. By the Right Rev. J. W. Colenso, D.D. Bishop of Natal. Crown 8vo. 6s.

An INTRODUCTION to the STUDY of the NEW TESTAMENT, Critical, Exegetical, and Theological. By the Rev. S. Davidson, D.D. LL.D. 2 vols. 8vo. price 30s.

SOME QUESTIONS of the DAY. By the Author of ' Amy Herbert.' Crown 8vo. price 2s. 6d.

THOUGHTS for the AGE. By the Author of 'Amy Herbert,' &c. New Edition, revised. Fcp. 8vo. price 3s. 6d.

The DOCTRINE and PRACTICE of CONFESSION in the CHURCH of ENGLAND. By the Rev. W. E. Jelf, B.D. 8vo. price 7s. 6d.

PREPARATION for the HOLY COMMUNION; the Devotions chiefly from the Works of Jeremy Taylor. By Miss Sewell. 32mo. 3s.

LYRA GERMANICA, Hymns translated from the German by Miss C. Winkworth. Fcp. 8vo. price 5s.

SPIRITUAL SONGS for the SUNDAYS and HOLIDAYS through-out the Year. By J. S. B. Monsell, LL.D. Ninth Thousand. Fcp. 8vo. 5s. 18mo. 2s.

ENDEAVOURS after the CHRISTIAN LIFE: Discourses. By the Rev. J. Martineau, LL.D. Fifth Edition, carefully revised. Crown 8vo. 7s. 6d.

HYMNS of PRAISE and PRAYER, collected and edited by the Rev. J. Martineau, LL.D. Crown 8vo. 4s. 6d. 32mo. 1s. 6d.

The TYPES of GENESIS, briefly considered as revealing the Development of Human Nature. By Andrew Jukes. Third Edition. Crown 8vo. 7s. 6d.

The SECOND DEATH and the RESTITUTION of ALL THINGS; with some Preliminary Remarks on the Nature and Inspiration of Holy Scripture. By Andrew Jukes. Fourth Edition. Crown 8vo. 3s. 6d.

WHATELY'S INTRODUCTORY LESSONS on the CHRISTIAN Evidences. 18mo. 6d.

BISHOP JEREMY TAYLOR'S ENTIRE WORKS. With Life by Bishop Heber. Revised and corrected by the Rev. C. P. Eden. Complete in Ten Volumes, 8vo. cloth, price £5. 5s.

Travels, Voyages, &c.

The INDIAN ALPS, and How we Crossed them: being a Narrative of Two Years' Residence in the Eastern Himalayas, and Two Months' Tour into the Interior, towards Kinchinjunga and Mount Everest. By a Lady Pioneer. With Illustrations from Original Drawings made on the spot by the Authoress. Imperial 8vo. 42s.

TYROL and the TYROLESE; being an Account of the People and the Land, in their Social, Sporting, and Mountaineering Aspects. By W. A. BAILLIE GROHMAN. With numerous Illustrations from Sketches by the Author. Crown 8vo. 14s.

'The FROSTY CAUCASUS;' An Account of a Walk through Part of the Range, and of an Ascent of Elbruz in the Summer of 1874. By F. C. GROVE. With Eight Illustrations engraved on Wood by E. Whymper, from Photographs taken during the Journey, and a Map. Crown 8vo. price 15s.

A JOURNEY of 1,000 MILES through EGYPT and NUBIA to the SECOND CATARACT of the NILE. By AMELIA B. EDWARDS. With numerous Illustrations from Drawings by the Authoress, Map, Plans, Facsimiles, &c. Imperial 8vo.   [In the Autumn.

OVER the SEA and FAR AWAY; being a Narrative of a Ramble round the World. By THOMAS WOODBINE HINCHLIFF, M.A. F.R.G.S. President of the Alpine Club, Author of 'Summer Months among the Alps.' With 14 full-page Illustrations, engraved on Wood from Photographs and Sketches. Medium 8vo. 21s.

THROUGH BOSNIA and the HERZEGOVINA on FOOT during the INSURRECTION, August and September 1875; with an Historical Review of Bosnia, and a Glimpse at the Croats, Slavonians, and the Ancient Republic of Ragusa. By A. J. EVANS, B.A. F.S.A. With Map and 58 Wood Engravings from Photographs and Sketches by the Author. 8vo. 18s.

DISCOVERIES at EPHESUS, including the Site and Remains of the Great Temple of Diana. By J. T. WOOD, F.S.A. 1 vol. Imperial 8vo. copiously illustrated.   [In the press.

MEMORIALS of the DISCOVERY and EARLY SETTLEMENT of the BERMUDAS or SOMERS ISLANDS, from 1515 to 1685. Compiled from the Colonial Records and other original sources. By Major-General J. H. LEFROY, R.A. C.B. F.R.S. &c. Governor of the Bermudas. 8vo. with Map.   [In the press.

ITALIAN ALPS; Sketches in the Mountains of Ticino, Lombardy, the Trentino, and Venetia. By DOUGLAS W. FRESHFIELD, Editor of 'The Alpine Journal.' Square crown 8vo. with Maps and Illustrations, price 15s.

The RIFLE and the HOUND in CEYLON. By Sir SAMUEL W. BAKER, M.A. F.R.G.S. New Edition, with Illustrations engraved on Wood by G. Pearson. Crown 8vo. 7s. 6d.

EIGHT YEARS in CEYLON. By Sir SAMUEL W. BAKER, M.A. F.R.G.S. New Edition, with Illustrations engraved on Wood, by G. Pearson. Crown 8vo. 7s. 6d.

TWO YEARS IN FIJI, a Descriptive Narrative of a Residence in the Fijian Group of Islands; with some Account of the Fortunes of Foreign Settlers and Colonists up to the Time of the British Annexation. By LITTON FORBES, M.D. F.R.G.S. Crown 8vo. 8s. 6d.

MEETING the SUN; a Journey all round the World through Egypt, China, Japan, and California. By WILLIAM SIMPSON, F.R.G.S. With 48 Heliotypes and Wood Engravings from Drawings by the Author. Medium 8vo. 24s.

UNTRODDEN PEAKS and UNFREQUENTED VALLEYS; a Midsummer Ramble among the Dolomites. By AMELIA B. EDWARDS. With a Map and 27 Wood Engravings. Medium 8vo. 21s.

The DOLOMITE MOUNTAINS; Excursions through Tyrol, Carinthia, Carniola, and Friuli, 1861-1863. By J. GILBERT and G. C. CHURCHILL, F.R.G.S. With numerous Illustrations. Square crown 8vo. 21s.

The ALPINE CLUB MAP of SWITZERLAND, with parts of the Neighbouring Countries, on the Scale of Four Miles to an Inch. Edited by R. C. NICHOLS, F.S.A. F.R.G.S. In Four Sheets, price 42s. or mounted in a case, 52s. 6d. Each Sheet may be had separately, price 12s. or mounted in a case, 15s.

MAP of the CHAIN of MONT BLANC, from an Actual Survey in 1863-1864. By ADAMS-REILLY, F.R.G.S. M.A.C. Published under the Authority of the Alpine Club. In Chromolithography on extra stout drawing-paper 28in. × 17in. price 10s. or mounted on canvas in a folding case, 12s. 6d.

HOW to SEE NORWAY. By Captain J. R. CAMPBELL. With Map and 5 Woodcuts. Fcp. 8vo. price 5s.

GUIDE to the PYRENEES, for the use of Mountaineers. By CHARLES PACKE. With Map and Illustrations. Crown 8vo. 7s. 6d.

The ALPINE GUIDE. By JOHN BALL, M.R.I.A. late President of the Alpine Club. 3 vols. post 8vo. Thoroughly Revised Editions, with Maps and Illustrations:—I. Western Alps, 6s. 6d. II. Central Alps, 7s. 6d. III. Eastern Alps, 10s. 6d. Or in Ten Parts, price 2s. 6d. each.

Introduction on Alpine Travelling in General, and on the Geology of the Alps, price 1s. Each of the Three Volumes or Parts of the Alpine Guide may be had with this INTRODUCTION prefixed, price 1s. extra.

Works of Fiction.

HIGGLEDY-PIGGLEDY; or, Stories for Everybody and Everybody's Children. By the Right Hon. E. M. KNATCHBULL-HUGESSEN, M.P. With Nine Illustrations from Original Designs by R. Doyle, engraved on Wood by G. Pearson. Crown 8vo. price 6s.

WHISPERS from FAIRYLAND. By the Right Hon. E. H. KNATCH-BULL-HUGESSEN, M.P. With Nine Illustrations from Original Designs engraved on Wood by G. Pearson. Crown 8vo. price 6s.

NOVELS and TALES. By the Right Hon. B. DISRAELI, M.P. Cabinet Edition, complete in Ten Volumes, crown 8vo. price £3.

LOTHAIR, 6s.	HENRIETTA TEMPLE, 6s.
CONINGSBY, 6s.	CONTARINI FLEMING, &c. 6s.
SYBIL, 6s.	ALROY, IXION, &c. 6s.
TANCRED, 6s.	The YOUNG DUKE, &c. 6s.
VENETIA, 6s.	VIVIAN GREY 6s.

CABINET EDITION of STORIES and TALES by Miss SEWELL:—

AMY HERBERT, 2s. 6d.	IVORS, 2s. 6d.
GERTRUDE, 2s. 6d.	KATHARINE ASHTON, 2s. 6d
The EARL'S DAUGHTER, 2s. 6d.	MARGARET PERCIVAL, 3s. 6d.
EXPERIENCE of LIFE, 2s. 6d.	LANETON PARSONAGE, 3s. 6d.
CLEVE HALL, 2s. 6d.	URSULA, 3s. 6d.

BECKER'S GALLUS; or, Roman Scenes of the Time of Augustus: with Notes and Excursuses. New Edition. Post 8vo. 7s. 6d.

BECKER'S CHARICLES; a Tale illustrative of Private Life among the Ancient Greeks: with Notes and Excursuses. New Edition. Post 8vo. 7s. 6d.

The MODERN NOVELIST'S LIBRARY. Each Work, in crown 8vo.
complete in a Single Volume :—

ATHERSTONE PRIORY, 2s. boards ; 2s. 6d. cloth.
MADEMOISELLE MORI, 2s. boards ; 2s. 6d. cloth.
MELVILLE'S GLADIATORS, 2s boards ; 2s. 6d. cloth.
———— GOOD FOR NOTHING, 2s. boards ; 2s. 6d. cloth.
———— HOLMBY HOUSE, 2s. boards ; 2s. 6d. cloth.
———— INTERPRETER, 2s. boards ; 2s. 6d. cloth.
———— KATE COVENTRY, 2s. boards ; 2s. 6d. cloth.
———— QUEEN'S MARIES, 2s. boards ; 2s. 6d. cloth.
———— DIGBY GRAND, 2s. boards ; 2s. 6d. cloth.
———— GENERAL BOUNCE, 2s. boards ; 2s. 6d. cloth.
TROLLOPE'S WARDEN, 1s. 6d. boards ; 2s. cloth.
————BARCHESTER TOWERS, 2s. boards ; 2s. 6d. cloth.
BRAMLEY-MOORE'S SIX SISTERS *of the* VALLEYS, 2s. boards ; 2s. 6d. cloth.
The BURGOMASTER'S FAMILY, 2s. boards ; 2s. 6d. cloth.
ELSA, a Tale of the Tyrolean Alps. Translated from the German of WILHELMINE
    VON HILLERN by Lady WALLACE. 2s. boards ; 2s. 6d. cloth.

Poetry and *The Drama.*

POEMS. By WILLIAM B. SCOTT. I. Ballads and Tales. II. Studies
    from Nature. III. Sonnets &c. Illustrated by 17 Etchings by L. ALMA
    TADEMA and WILLIAM B. SCOTT. Crown 8vo. price 15s.

MOORE'S IRISH MELODIES, with 161 Steel Plates from Original
    Drawings by D. MACLISE, R.A. New Edition. Super-royal 8vo. 21s.

The LONDON SERIES of FRENCH CLASSICS. Edited by CH.
    CASSAL, LL.D. T. KARCHER, LL.B. and LÉONCE STIÉVENARD. In course of
    publication, in fcp. 8vo. volumes. The following Plays, in the Division of the
    Drama in this Series, are now ready :—

CORNEILLE'S LE CID, 1s. 6d.
CORNEILLE'S POLYEUCTE, 1s. 6d.
RACINE'S IPHIGÉNIE, 1s. 6d.
VOLTAIRE'S ZAÏRE, 1s. 6d.

VOLTAIRE'S ALZIRE, 1s. 6d.
LAMARTINE'S TOUSSAINT LOUVERTURE
    2s. 6d.
DE VIGNY'S CHATTERTON, 1s. 6d.

BALLADS and LYRICS of OLD FRANCE; with other Poems. By
    A. LANG, M.A. Late fellow of Merton College, Oxford. Square fcp. 8vo. 5s.

SOUTHEY'S POETICAL WORKS, with the Author's last Corrections
    and copyright Additions. Medium 8vo. with Portrait and Vignette, 14s.

LAYS of ANCIENT ROME; with IVRY and the ARMADA. By the
    Right Hon. Lord MACAULAY. 16mo. 3s. 6d.

LORD MACAULAY'S LAYS of ANCIENT ROME. With 90 Illustra-
    tions on Wood, from the Antique, from Drawings by G. SCHARF. Fcp. 4to. 21s.

Miniature Edition of Lord Macaulay's Lays of Ancient Rome,
    with the Illustrations (as above) reduced in Lithography. Imp. 16mo. 10s. 6d.

The ÆNEID of VIRGIL Translated into English Verse. By JOHN
    CONINGTON, M.A. New Edition. Crown 8vo. 9s.

HORATII OPERA. Library Edition, with Marginal References and English Notes. Edited by the Rev. J. E. YONGE, M.A. 8vo. 21s.

The LYCIDAS and EPITAPHIUM DAMONIS of MILTON. Edited, with Notes and Introduction (including a Reprint of the rare Latin Version of the Lycidas, by W. Hogg, 1694), by C. S. JERRAM, M.A. Crown 8vo. 2s. 6d.

BOWDLER'S FAMILY SHAKSPEARE, cheaper Genuine Editions. Medium 8vo. large type, with 36 WOODCUTS, price 14s. Cabinet Edition, with the same ILLUSTRATIONS, 6 vols. fcp. 8vo. price 21s.

POEMS. By JEAN INGELOW. 2 vols. fcp. 8vo. price 10s.
FIRST SERIES, containing ' DIVIDED,' ' The STAR'S MONUMENT,' &c. Sixteenth Thousand. Fcp. 8vo. price 5s.
SECOND SERIES, 'A STORY of DOOM,' 'GLADYS and her ISLAND,' &c. Fifth Thousand. Fcp. 8vo. price 5s.

POEMS by Jean Ingelow. FIRST SERIES, with nearly 100 Illustrations, engraved on Wood by Dalziel Brothers. Fcp. 4to. 21s.

Rural Sports, &c.

DOWN the ROAD; Or, Reminiscences of a Gentleman Coachman. By C. T. S. BIRCH REYNARDSON. Second Edition, with Twelve Coloured Illustrations from Paintings by H. Alken. Medium 8vo. 21s.

ANNALS of the ROAD; Or, Notes on Mail and Stage Coaching in Great Britain. By CAPTAIN MALET, 18th Hussars. To which are added, Essays on the Road, by NIMROD. With 3 Woodcuts and 10 Illustrations in Chromo-lithography. Medium 8vo. 21s.

ENCYCLOPÆDIA of RURAL SPORTS; a complete Account, Historical, Practical, and Descriptive, of Hunting, Shooting, Fishing, Racing, and all other Rural and Athletic Sports and Pastimes. By D. P. BLAINE. With above 600 Woodcuts (20 from Designs by JOHN LEECH). 8vo. 21s.

The FLY-FISHER'S ENTOMOLOGY. By ALFRED RONALDS. With coloured Representations of the Natural and Artificial Insect. Sixth Edition, with 20 coloured Plates. 8vo. 14s.

A BOOK on ANGLING; a complete Treatise on the Art of Angling in every branch. By FRANCIS FRANCIS. New Edition, with Portrait and 15 other Plates, plain and coloured. Post 8vo. 15s.

WILCOCKS'S SEA-FISHERMAN ; comprising the Chief Methods of Hook and Line Fishing, a Glance at Nets, and Remarks on Boats and Boating. New Edition, with 80 Woodcuts. Post 8vo. 12s. 6d.

HORSES and STABLES. By Colonel F. FITZWYGRAM, XV. the King's Hussars. With Twenty-four Plates of Illustrations, containing very numerous Figures engraved on Wood. 8vo. 10s. 6d.

The HORSE'S FOOT, and HOW to KEEP it SOUND. By W. MILES, Esq. Ninth Edition, with Illustrations. Imperial 8vo. 12s. 6d.

A PLAIN TREATISE on HORSE-SHOEING. By W. MILES, Esq. Sixth Edition. Post 8vo. with Illustrations, 2s. 6d.

STABLES and **STABLE-FITTINGS.** By W. Miles, Esq. Imp. 8vo.
with 13 Plates, 15s.

REMARKS on **HORSES' TEETH,** addressed to Purchasers. By W.
Miles, Esq. Post 8vo. 1s. 6d.

The **HORSE:** with a Treatise on Draught. By William Youatt.
New Edition, revised and enlarged. 8vo. with numerous Woodcuts, 12s. 6d.

The **DOG.** By William Youatt. 8vo. with numerous Woodcuts, 6s.

The **DOG** in **HEALTH** and **DISEASE.** By Stonehenge. With 70
Wood Engravings. Square crown 8vo. 7s. 6d.

The **GREYHOUND.** By Stonehenge. Revised Edition, with 25
Portraits of Greyhounds. Square crown 8vo. 15s.

The **OX**; his **Diseases** and their **Treatment**: with an Essay on Parturi-
tion in the Cow. By J. R. Dobson. Crown 8vo. with Illustrations, 7s. 6d.

Works of *Utility* and *General Information.*

The **THEORY** and **PRACTICE** of **BANKING.** By H. D. Macleod,
M.A. Barrister-at-Law. Third Edition, thoroughly revised. 2 vols. 8vo.
price 26s.

The **ELEMENTS** of **BANKING.** By Henry Dunning Macleod,
Esq. M.A. of Trinity College, Cambridge, and the Inner Temple, Barrister-at-
Law. Crown 8vo. price 7s. 6d.

M'CULLOCH'S DICTIONARY, Practical, Theoretical, and Historical,
of Commerce and Commercial Navigation. New and revised Edition. 8vo. 63s.
Supplement, price 5s.

The **CABINET LAWYER**; a Popular Digest of the Laws of England,
Civil, Criminal, and Constitutional: intended for Practical Use and General
Information. Twenty-fifth Edition. Fcp. 8vo. price 9s.

BLACKSTONE ECONOMISED, a Compendium of the Laws of
England to the Present time, in Four Books, each embracing the Legal Principles
and Practical Information contained in their respective volumes of Blackstone,
supplemented by Subsequent Statutory Enactments, Important Legal Decisions,
&c. By D. M. Aird, Barrister-at-Law. Revised Edition. Post 8vo. 7s. 6d.

PEWTNER'S COMPREHENSIVE SPECIFIER; a Guide to the
Practical Specification of every kind of Building-Artificers' Work, with Forms
of Conditions and Agreements. Edited by W. Young. Crown 8vo. 6s.

WILLICH'S POPULAR TABLES for ascertaining according to the
Carlisle Table of Mortality the Value of Lifehold, Leasehold, and Church Property,
Renewal Fines, Reversions, &c.; also Interest, Legacy, Succession Duty, and
various other useful Tables. Eighth Edition. Post 8vo. 10s.

HINTS to **MOTHERS** on the **MANAGEMENT** of their **HEALTH**
during the Period of Pregnancy and in the Lying-in Room. By the late
Thomas Bull, M.D. Fcp. 8vo. 5s.

The MATERNAL MANAGEMENT of CHILDREN in HEALTH and
Disease. By the late THOMAS BULL, M.D. Fcp. 8vo. 5s.

The THEORY of the MODERN SCIENTIFIC GAME of WHIST.
By WILLIAM POLE, F.R.S. Seventh Edition, enlarged. Fcp. 8vo. 2s. 6d.

The CORRECT CARD; or, How to Play at Whist: a Whist Catechism.
By Captain A. CAMPBELL-WALKER, F.R.G.S. late 79th Highlanders; Author of
'The Rifle, its Theory and Practice.' 32mo, 2s. 6d.

CHESS OPENINGS. By F. W. LONGMAN, Balliol College, Oxford.
Second Edition revised. Fcp. 8vo. 2s. 6d.

THREE HUNDRED ORIGINAL CHESS PROBLEMS and STUDIES.
By JAMES PIERCE, M.A. and W. T. PIERCE. With numerous Diagrams. Square
fcp. 8vo. 7s. 6d. SUPPLEMENT, price 2s. 6d.

A SKETCH of the HISTORY of TAXES in ENGLAND from the
Earliest Times to the Present Day. By STEPHEN DOWELL. Vol. I. to the Civil
War 1642. 8vo. 10s. 6d.

The NEW CODE of the Education Department, with Notes, Analysis,
Appendix, and Index, and a Sketch of the Administration of the Grants for
Public Elementary Education (1839–1876). By H. J. GIBBS, and J. W. EDWARDS,
Barrister-at-Law. Second Edition, revised and adapted to the New Code, 1876.
Crown 8vo. 3s. 6d.

A PRACTICAL TREATISE on BREWING; with Formulæ for Public
Brewers, and Instructions for Private Families. By W. BLACK. 8vo. 10s. 6d.

MODERN COOKERY for PRIVATE FAMILIES, reduced to a System
of Easy Practice in a Series of carefully-tested Receipts. By ELIZA ACTON.
Newly revised and enlarged; with 8 Plates and 150 Woodcuts. Fcp. 8vo. 6s.

MAUNDER'S TREASURY of KNOWLEDGE and LIBRARY of
Reference; comprising an English Dictionary and Grammar, Universal Gazetteer,
Classical Dictionary, Chronology, Law Dictionary, a synopsis of the Peerage
useful Tables, &c. Revised Edition. Fcp. 8vo. 6s. cloth, or 10s. 6d. calf.

Knowledge for the *Young.*

The STEPPING-STONE to KNOWLEDGE; or upwards of 700
Questions and Answers on Miscellaneous Subjects, adapted to the capacity of
Infant minds. New Edition, revised. 18mo. 1s.

SECOND SERIES of the STEPPING-STONE to KNOWLEDGE:
Containing upwards of 800 Questions and Answers on Miscellaneous Subjects
not contained in the FIRST SERIES. 18mo. 1s.

The STEPPING-STONE to GEOGRAPHY: Containing several
Hundred Questions and Answers on Geographical Subjects. 18mo. 1s.

The STEPPING-STONE to ENGLISH HISTORY; Questions and
Answers on the History of England. 18mo. 1s.

The STEPPING-STONE to BIBLE KNOWLEDGE; Questions and Answers on the Old and New Testaments. 18mo. 1s.

The STEPPING-STONE to BIOGRAPHY; Questions and Answers on the Lives of Eminent Men and Women. 18mo. 1s.

The STEPPING-STONE to IRISH HISTORY: Containing several Hundred Questions and Answers on the History of Ireland. 18mo. 1s.

The STEPPING-STONE to FRENCH HISTORY: Containing several Hundred Questions and Answers on the History of France. 18mo. 1s.

The STEPPING-STONE to ROMAN HISTORY: Containing several Hundred Questions and Answers on the History of Rome. 18mo. 1s.

The STEPPING-STONE to GRECIAN HISTORY: Containing several Hundred Questions and Answers on the History of Greece. 18mo. 1s.

The STEPPING-STONE to ENGLISH GRAMMAR: Containing several Hundred Questions and Answers on English Grammar. 18mo. 1s.

The STEPPING-STONE to FRENCH PRONUNCIATION and CON-VERSATION : Containing several Hundred Questions and Answers. 18mo. 1s.

The STEPPING-STONE to ASTRONOMY: Containing several Hundred familiar Questions and Answers on the Earth and the Solar and Stellar Systems. 18mo. 1s.

The STEPPING-STONE to MUSIC: Containing several Hundred Questions on the Science; also a short History of Music. 18mo. 1s.

The STEPPING-STONE to NATURAL HISTORY: VERTEBRATE OR BACK-BONED ANIMALS. PART I. *Mammalia*; PART II. *Birds, Reptiles, and Fishes.* 18mo. 1s. each Part.

THE STEPPING-STONE to ARCHITECTURE; Questions and Answers explaining the Principles and Progress of Architecture from the Earliest Times. With 100 Woodcuts. 18mo. 1s.

INDEX.

Spottiswoode & Co., Printers, New-street Square, London.

www.ingramcontent.com/pod-product-compliance
Lightning Source LLC
Chambersburg PA
CBHW030120030726

47498CB00007B/2468